SELECTED POEMS AND
PROSE OF
JOHN CLARE

SELECTED POEMS AND
PROSE OF
JOHN CLARE

Chosen and edited by Eric Robinson
and Geoffrey Summerfield

With wood-engravings by David Gentleman

OXFORD   LONDON   NEW YORK

OXFORD UNIVERSITY PRESS

Oxford University Press, Walton Street, Oxford OX2 6DP

OXFORD LONDON GLASGOW
NEW YORK TORONTO MELBOURNE WELLINGTON
IBADAN NAIROBI DAR ES SALAAM LUSAKA CAPE TOWN
KUALA LUMPUR SINGAPORE JAKARTA HONG KONG TOKYO
DELHI BOMBAY CALCUTTA MADRAS KARACHI

CASEBOUND ISBN 0 19 212164 2
PAPERBACK ISBN 0 19 281232 7

Introduction and Glossary
first published in Clare: Selected Poems and Prose
New Oxford English Series, 1966

Poems and Prose
© *Eric Robinson 1967*

First issued as an Oxford Paperback 1978

Printed in Great Britain
at the University Press, Oxford
by Vivian Ridler
Printer to the University

ACKNOWLEDGEMENTS

WE WISH to thank the Peterborough Museum Society and the Northampton Public Library Committee for permission to publish from their extensive collections of Clare manuscripts, and we owe a special debt to Dr. Alexander Bell at Peterborough and to Mr. Howard Halliday, Northampton Public Librarian, and his staff, for their enthusiasm and helpfulness over many years.

The copyright of Clare's unpublished works is owned by Mr. Eric Robinson.

ERIC ROBINSON
GEOFFREY SUMMERFIELD

CONTENTS

The titles of poems are Clare's except when given in
square brackets

viii

x

INTRODUCTION

IN every generation since 1820, when Clare's first book of poetry was published by John Taylor, the publisher of Keats and Lamb, and received considerable though condescending acclaim from the reviewers, there have been some who have listened attentively to his distinctive voice. But while the names of Keats and Shelley, Wordsworth, Coleridge, and Byron continue to resound in the annals of criticism, Clare still struggles for a hearing with the general public and even in the university schools of literary study. The old *Oxford Book of English Verse* preserved 'I am' (p. 195) from oblivion, while the school anthologies for very young children kept alive 'Little Trotty Wagtail' and perhaps one or two other lyrics from the poet's declining years. But collections of Clare's prose and verse, affording a truer perspective of his genius, generally sold slowly and could often be found among remaindered books. Perceptive critics like Edward Thomas, Edmund Blunden, J. Middleton Murry, and Geoffrey Grigson and Robert Graves[1] have made a beginning, in this century, in the serious criticism of Clare's poetry, but there is still no single critical work devoted to Clare, and to many students of poetry he remains unknown. Yet Clare is a great poet, and no small part of his greatness is, as Robert Graves has shown, that he held firmly to his poetic vision throughout a long life, while some like Wordsworth and Southey faltered, and others like Keats and Shelley died very young. Inertia is a dreadful natural force. Southey, who is read even less than Clare, is firmly enshrined by the encyclopaedias and literary histories in the Pantheon, while Clare, probably more happy there, is pottering about in the garden outside.

Yet Clare is the most accessible of poets, because he is free of pretension and almost always writes about the things he knows well and which are a part of his life. Apart from a few short visits to London and his brief confinement in the asylum at High Beech in Epping Forest, he spent almost his entire life in his native county of Northamptonshire. Even there, in that one county, his whole experience centred on the years of his childhood and early manhood

[1] See Select Bibliography.

in the little village of Helpstone. Thus the whole of his spiritual life is in a sense confined to within a day's walking distance in every direction radiating from Helpstone, though there are a few topographical poems about Boston Stump and other places in the neighbouring county of Lincolnshire. Since he came to be known as 'the Northamptonshire Peasant Poet', Clare was doubly damned from the beginning—damned because he was associated with one locality at a time when the railways were breaking down regional boundaries and regional consciousness; and damned because he was a peasant at a time when the national imagination was being captured by the immensity of industrialism. Wordsworth's allegiance to rural Cumberland was first trumpeted a generation before Clare's first volume, and perhaps was easily acceptable because it came from a man of education and could be seen as part of a literary convention. But Clare was not only loyal to the countryside, he was part of it—a whopstraw, another Robert Bloomfield, smelling of the farmyard.

Much of Clare's strength, however, lies in his sense of his roots, his awareness of his own landscape, the directness with which he always sees the places of his childhood. The poem 'Remembrances' (p. 174) brings together many of the places which, elsewhere in Clare's work, earned a poem or poems to themselves. In this poem, however, they are used as a sort of incantation whose power can only be fully appreciated after much browsing in Clare's very extensive poetic output. Langley bush, Eastwell's boiling spring, old Cross Berry way, pleasant Swordy Well, the hollow ash, Sneap Green, Puddocks Nook, Hilly Snow; they are not names alone to Clare, but experiences. Some of these places can still be located on enclosure maps, and even on the modern ordnance maps, but other landmarks, such as trees, have succumbed to time. One tree, however, which can still be pinpointed is 'Salter's Tree' (p. 163) which grew near Castor, but Clare's poetry is full of regrets for other well-known trees that fell to the axe, just as the moorlands were devoured by the plough or the streams were diverted from their natural course in the interests of improved farming, Clare's memory for persons and places was the memory of a saga-teller. There is a letter written from Northampton Asylum in which he asks to be remembered to all the friends of his youth in Helpstone, and the names come flooding from his pen as though he were standing before their cottages and calling them out. Because his vision is always so sharp, whether he writes about a person or a bird's nest, and his memory so reliable, there is a strength in his poetry which seldom allows him to become merely sentimental.

But places have a deeper significance in Clare's poetry than the places that most of us would think of as our map of childhood from which, if we rack our memories, we can remember the name of the street in which we lived, the field where we lit our first illicit bonfire, or the lanes along which we strolled to school. For the map was changed for Helpstone, as well as for many more midland villages, not only by time but also by enclosure. The 'landscape plotted and pieced', about which Hopkins wrote in the later nineteenth century, was largely the product of eighteenth-century and early nineteenth-century enclosure. And so Clare lamented:

> But now alls fled and flats of many a dye
> That seemed to lengthen with the following eye
> Moors loosing from the sight far smooth and blea
> Where swept the plover in its pleasure free
> Are vanished now with commons wild and gay . . .
>
> (*The Mores*, p. 169)

Enclosure changed the landscape, and, in Clare's opinion, destroyed a way of life, not only by tearing up trees and damming brooks, but also by uprooting old customs and changing the social links between master and man. His long satiric poem, *The Parish*, from which we have only space for a few short extracts, is taken up with the evil social effects of enclosure, the inflationary agriculture of the Napoleonic Wars, and the changed status of the local Anglican parson. Even if he were not a fine poet, Clare's observations would be of great value to the historian, since his is almost the only voice that can still be heard from the otherwise silent peasantry of the enclosure years. Even Cobbett, close as his observation is, wrote as a comparative outsider. Clare's remarks help to explain why Anglicanism suffered some of its most severe setbacks in the very rural areas where it might have been expected to be strongest.[1] Similarly, Clare's observations on the old Poor Law institutions of his neighbourhood show them to have possessed much of the severity often said to be the consequence of the Poor Law Reform Act of 1834. As for the customs and the social structure of the early nineteenth-century Northamptonshire village, there is no historical work which could possibly bring them to life as

[1] W. R. Ward, 'The Tithe Question in England in the Early Nineteenth Century', *Journal of Ecclesiastical History*, xvi. 1, 1965.

vividly as some of Clare's poems and prose passages do. (See below; 'Valentine Eve', pp. 55–64, 'The Cellar Door', pp. 46–50, 'A Sunday with Shepherds and Herdboys', pp. 94–98, and the long passage about the Farmer and the Vicar, pp. 24–30.) Moreover certain sides of peasant life in Clare's period could only be appreciated fully by someone with first-hand knowledge like his. Thus, for example, while it is true that enclosure afforded additional employment in hedging and ditching, Clare, who worked as a member of a gang planting new quick-set hedges, knew from personal experience that it was no job for a married man, because it was itinerant and forced him to sleep abroad, sometimes even in the fields. The hero of his poem, 'Valentine Eve', poses as a wandering Irish harvest worker:

> When the poor irish from their country roves
> And like scotch cattle throng the road in droves

How much social and economic history is concentrated in those two lines, with their reference to migrant Irish farm labour and to the Scottish cattle trade.[1] Clare not only observed his environment but had the wit to know what was significant in it, so that to the discerning eye there is a greater width of reference in his verse and prose than he has ever been given credit for. The famous social historians, the Hammonds, were not at fault in quoting from Clare in their classic *The Village Labourer*, but only in not quoting enough, though it must be remembered that they only knew what had been published of Clare's work in 1911.

If the countryside about Helpstone was not only the map of Clare's boyhood but also part of a rural landscape cruelly altered by enclosure, it was something even more significant. Helpstone was Clare's Paradise, his Garden of Eden. This observation is no literary conceit but plain truth. There is a similarity here between Wordsworth's philosophy in the 'Ode on the Intimations of Immortality' and Clare's imaginative position; but Clare goes much further than Wordsworth in actually identifying the fields of his boyhood with Eden—even, he says, with something more than Eden:

> I sat beside the pasture stream
> When Beautys self was sitting by
> The fields did more than Eden seem
> Nor could I tell the reason why

[1] For one of the finest contemporary descriptions of a Scotch drover, see E. Robinson and G. Summerfield (edd.), *John Clare: The Shepherd's Calendar*, (Oxford, 1964), pp. 76–77.

In the landscape of Eden before the Fall, Clare's boyhood love, Mary Joyce, is present—she is the Eve to Clare's Adam. Unless we recognize that this is the conscious pattern of imagery in Clare's poetry, we are bound to miss a great deal of his point. Everything in his boyhood environment assumes a new character, a vividness far beyond accurate natural history, a deeper identity because it is part of what Clare calls 'Loves register'. In this 'register', not just trees but every single tree, not just grass but every single blade of grass is a special act of the Creator and participates in the freshness before the Fall. This is where Middleton Murry, one of the best critics of Clare, goes astray, when, writing of the differences between Clare and Wordsworth, he says that Clare in some ways was a truer poet than Wordsworth, because he had

a truer ear and a more exquisite instinct for words; *but he had nothing of the principle of inward growth which gives to Wordsworth's most careless work a place within the unity of a great scheme.* Wordsworth's incessant effort to comprehend experience would itself have been incomprehensible to Clare.[1]

Wordsworth's effort would not have been incomprehensible to Clare because he had made, himself, the same effort. This can best be seen by examining Clare's poetry extensively, but it can be illustrated, to a limited degree, in this selection also. Thus, in 'Shadows of Taste', he writes:

> Some in recordless rapture love to breath[e]
> Natures wild Eden wood and field and heath   (p. 112)

and in 'The Morning Wind':

> Theres more then music in this early wind
> Awaking like a bird refreshed from sleep
> And joy what Adam might in eden find
> When he with angels did communion keep   (p. 153)

The daisies, he tells us, in 'The Flitting' (p. 176) are as old as Adam and were there when the earth first beheld the sun. Sometimes the allusions to this Eden are explicit, but quite often it is the sharpness of Clare's vision alone that serves to remind us of the 'great scheme' to which his experience belonged.

[1] J. Middleton Murry, *Countries of the Mind*, London, 1937, p. 71. Our italics.

The recognition of Clare's effort to comprehend his experience in a scheme of imagery would have come more quickly if critics had been more humble towards him. Instead, they have too often stressed Clare's lack of education and his village upbringing, and so have mesmerized themselves into believing that Clare was incapable of sustained thought. But, to put it in the simplest terms, Clare was very well read. His observations of nature often reminded him of his own reading. (See prose passage, p. 9.) He shared in that culture of the great house which descended by devious routes to the cottages, through servants and servants' servants, down to the very poor. It produced not only a society of good manners but also here and there the man and woman of humble station who had read more than the three or four great classics of the cottage shelf—the Bible, *Paradise Lost, Pilgrim's Progress*, and *Robinson Crusoe*. Clare's friends among the servants at the Fitzwilliam residence at Milton included Artis and Henderson, who were men of considerable culture, well read in their master's great library, and keenly interested in the antiquities and the natural history of the locality. He was accepted by them as their intellectual equal and they all shared many discoveries together, as well as lending each other books. Clare's library, or the greater part of it, still exists in Northampton Public Library,[1] and there is many an educated man today who possesses a poorer collection of books. Not only was he comparatively *widely* read in the English poetry of the eighteenth century, and in some of the poetry of the seventeenth century, but he was *deeply* read. What he read he made part of himself. His favourite authors, Thomson and Cowper, together with the Bible, may well have provided him with the framework of his ideas about Eden, but he carried those ideas into his own village fields. It may be natural for a shepherd to compare himself to the Jewish pastoralist of the Scriptures, and it was also a fairly common literary comparison in eighteenth-century poetry, but Clare gives life to the commonplace, and writes of sheep-shearing in June with the familiarity that lends authority to his description of social amity at the sheep-shearing feast.[2] In this way, reading and experience go hand in hand, as they do in Shakespeare's *The Winter's Tale*.

[1] D. Powell, *Catalogue of the John Clare Collection in the Northampton Public Library*, Northampton, 1964, pp. 23–34.
[2] See his *Shepherd's Calendar*, pp. 65–67.

While enclosure brought a sense of alienation to village life, Clare's own stability, mental and physical, was threatened by a number of personal factors, of which the two most important were the separation from Mary Joyce, and later, the move from Helpstone to Northborough. We cannot be certain why Clare and Mary parted, but it looks as if her father felt that Clare was her social inferior and that the relationship ought to be broken. Clare does not seem to have held Mary herself quite blameless in the matter, though his attitude varies in different poems. However that may be, Mary remained for the rest of his days the symbol of innocence, the Eve of his Eden, the First Love which was to be the touchstone for all later experience. That is why we have made 'Dedication to Mary' the first poem of this book. When he went mad, Clare believed that he was married to Mary, as well as to his real wife, Patty, and that he was imprisoned because of his bigamy. His love for Mary did not cause him to hate Patty (whose proper name was Martha Turner), but he regarded the two women as the Mary and Martha, in a scriptural sense, of his life. He wrote many poems to Mary, long after they had parted, and even long after she was dead, but did we not know this from other evidence, the poems would give us no hint of this fantastic situation. We might conclude from them that Clare was in fact married to Mary and was writing the poems to his living wife. But this is only of biographical interest: what is more important from the literary point of view is that Mary always elicits the very best from Clare's pen. The intense vision of some of Clare's asylum poems derives from Mary (see below, p. 194), and even when he writes, as he often does, of other girls, one can see that it is really Mary who inspires him. No other poet has ever managed to preserve inviolate the image of first love as Clare contrived to do, and for this reason alone he deserves a special place in the affections of the young. The earlier poems to Mary show the poet struggling to reconcile himself to the separation from her and to his deep sense of loss, but when all his other troubles of poverty, uprooting, and lack of public recognition fell upon him, his mind was unable to keep separate at all times the world of reality and the world of his soul's longing, in which Mary still lived and still was his.

Mary and Helpstone, Nature before enclosure, Eve before the Temptation, Eden before the Fall, childhood before the onset of adult trials and deceptions, were therefore a unity in Clare's mind.

Clare lived to experience a constant struggle between his vision of unity and all the discordant realities which broke it down, and which seemed in consequence to threaten the meaning of his existence. His first success came to him when his first volume of poetry was published in 1820, but that success was soured by the fact that Mary was no longer there to share it with him. Consoling himself with Martha Turner, he made her pregnant, and his sense of responsibility led him to marry her. She remained illiterate to the end of her days, always signing her name with a mark, and there are several indications that Clare did not always consider his wife and himself to be well suited to each other. Nevertheless she bore him several children and faced many years of hardship with him and without him. But the marriage did not begin auspiciously, and Clare had at least one other affair after his marriage. In addition, Clare's relationships with his patrons and his publishers were far from happy. Lord Radstock, an active, proselytizing Evangelical, helped Clare with great energy, but also bombarded him with comments on how he should conduct his spiritual life, his obligations to the opulent classes, and the ingratitude of his criticizing those in authority. 'I must confess that I discover in his character a want of gratitude and proper feeling towards the opulent and higher orders which has lower'd him not a little in my opinion': Radstock to Taylor, 30 March 1820. Clare resented his interference but was too much at a social disadvantage to remonstrate with his patron. He was reluctantly obliged to defer in several matters to him and to Radstock's friend, Mrs. Emmerson, whose rather silly emendations are littered over quite a number of Clare's manuscripts. In particular, Radstock and Mrs. Emmerson strongly objected to the vulgarity of Clare's muse—a vulgarity which in fact reflects a certain healthy robustness. John Taylor, the publisher, felt entitled to correct Clare's grammar, his rhyme-schemes, and his vocabulary, so that they would accord with the polite taste of the period. He was probably doing the only thing possible at the time, since this was a period, after 1820, when standards of correctness in spelling and grammar were becoming more stringent, but the consequences were severe, as we can better appreciate today. In the early volumes of Clare's poetry, Taylor was persuaded to allow many of Clare's dialect words to stand where they did not offend propriety, but by the time of *The Shepherd's Calendar* in 1827, the publisher was slashing more vigorously, until almost all Clare's 'provincialisms' were replaced by words acceptable to London literary taste.[1] Clare, however, was very much a son of his own village, as we have seen, and it was therefore natural for him to use the vocabulary of his everyday speech, especially when it was so much more telling than the poeticisms of his day. He strongly resented Taylor's treatment of the language of *The Shepherd's Calendar*,[2] and it is ironic that two present-day editors of Clare should write approvingly of Taylor's truncated version:

There are very few dialect words in the *Shepherd's Calendar*, and we find this deliberate part of his art almost perfected . . .[3]

The problem arises as to the way in which Clare should be published today. In this volume we have neither corrected Clare's spelling, grammar, nor punctuation, but have contented ourselves with referring the reader to the glossary wherever we thought that there might be obscurity. Once the business of correction is begun there is no end, and the editor soon finds himself trying to rewrite Clare's verse for him, in order to make a rhyme-scheme fit in with some modified piece of grammar. Clare makes his views about grammar perfectly clear in a fragment from what appears to be an unpublished essay:

Those who have made grammer up into a system and cut it into classes and orders as the student does the animal or vegetable creation may be a fine recreation for schools but it becomes of no use towards making any one so far acquainted with it as to find it useful—it will only serve to puzzle and mislead to awe and intimidate instead of aiding and encouraging him therefore it pays nothing for the study

A person may be very clever at cutting trees and animals on paper but he is nothing as an artist and a person may be very clever at detecting faults in composition and yet in the writing of it may be a mere cypher him self and one that can do nothing

And such a one as Cobbet who has come boldly forward and not only assailed the outworks of such a pedantic garison but like a skilful general laid open its weakness to all deserves from praise for the use of his labour [more] then all the rest of the castle building grammarians put together for he plainly comes to this conclusion—that what ever is intellig[i]ble to others is grammer and what ever is commonsense is not far from correctness.

[1] See E. Robinson and G. Summerfield, 'John Taylor's Editing of Clare's *The Shepherd's Calendar*', *Review of English Studies*, New Series, xiv. 56, November 1963, pp. 359–69.   [2] See *R.E.S.* article cited above.
[3] J. W. and Anne Tibble, *Life of John Clare*, London, 1932, p. 293.

The verse is nearly always quite easy to understand. The prose is a little more difficult, because Clare omits full-stops and capital letters, so we have tried the experiment of leaving a gap between sentences. But Clare feels that the most important thing is what a writer has to say, and that if he sets out to say it clearly, the punctuation will look after itself:

do I write intelligable I am genneraly understood tho I do not use that awkward squad of pointings called commas colons semicolons etc and for the very reason that altho they are drilled hourly daily and weekly by every boarding school Miss who pretends to gossip in correspondence they do not know their proper exercise for they even set gramarians at loggerheads and no one can assign them the proper places for give each a sentence to point and both shall differ—point it differently

What could be plainer than that? And see how cunningly the comparison with an awkward squad at drill is sustained through the passage. Clare's 'Journey out of Essex' (see below pp. 184–91) is an exemplary piece of direct writing, composed by a man worn out by physical and mental exertion, and the other prose passages in this book are intended to exemplify Clare's qualities as a prose writer. His sense of character and his ability to describe human relationships are shown in the passage about the Farmer and the Vicar (p. 24), his vigour of expression can perhaps be best appreciated in the Cobbett-like 'Apology for the Poor' (p. 171), while every passage of nature description exemplifies his accuracy and directness of evocation. Clare always objected strongly to artificiality of language in poetry and in prose. He objected, for example, to Shenstone's poems on the grounds that 'Putting the Correct Langauge of the Gentleman into the mouth of a Simple Shepherd or Vulgar Ploughman is far from Natural'.[1] His own writings are free from this vice, and are as innocent of pretension as they are of punctuation. His qualities are well displayed in his letters, where simplicity of style gives warmth and life to everything he writes, and when he chose to follow Gilbert White in adopting the letter as his vehicle for writing about natural history, he made a very wise choice.

To the separation from Mary, and to the difficulties which Clare increasingly experienced with his patrons and his publisher, must be

[1] J. W. and Anne Tibble (edd.), *Letters of John Clare*, London, 1951, p. 25.

added the change in taste of the English reading public in the eighteen-thirties. Taylor saw that there was a falling-off in the demand for poetry and wrote to Clare on 3 August 1827:

> The Season has been a very bad one for new Books, and I am afraid the Time has passed away in which Poetry will answer . . . the Shepherds Calendar has had comparatively no Sale . . . I think in future I shall confine my Speculations [i.e. financial] to works of Utility . . .[1]

Taylor began to specialize in textbooks of different kinds, and by 1830 had become bookseller and publisher to the University of London. The poet Darley wrote works on mathematics for him, and Taylor's list soon included numerous works on natural science and engineering, the intellectual tools of the Industrial Revolution. It is also probably true that the reading public wanted its literature to be increasingly *about* something, as a friend, to whom we are much indebted, illuminatingly comments in a letter to one of us:

> . . . the new town classes wanted books to be 'about' . . . and what was Clare 'about'? Nothing exciting like Walter Scott's nuns being walled up and Scotsmen dying at Flodden. Nothing exciting like Byron's Greeks. Nothing exciting like Keats' Italians . . . We were entering the world of the reviewers, who might have passed Clare if his dialect had reminded them of their Scottish home . . . He was not for girls—and they the readers of poetry—who saw soon they preferred the novel—high life seen from below stairs . . .[2]

New town habits were the death of Clare and his poetry as they were of Clare's world in general. It was a cruel twist of Fate that granted fame to an obscure agricultural labourer and then snatched it out of his grasp, as society, in its tormented sleep, turned its back on him. Taylor was blamed by Clare not only, rightly, for his lack of attention to Clare's concerns, but also, wrongly, for what was out of Taylor's control, a change of taste on the part of the reading public. Something of the change can be seen in the vogue for annuals,—'Keepsakes', 'Forget-Me-Nots', 'Friendship's Offerings' etc.,—which were shipped off to absent relatives in India or to maiden aunts in Lyme Regis, and to which Clare also submitted poems in the hope of earning an occasional half guinea. But man cannot live by candy-floss alone. Clare's family went short, he fell into debt, half-starved

---

[1] Taylor to Clare, 20 November 1827.
[2] E. Welbourne to E. Robinson, 25 June 1965.

himself, and became ill, and, as he thought, friendless. He could no longer return to village society, the shortcomings of which had always been clear to him

> Goosey goosey gander
> Where would you wander
> Up the fen and down the fen
> To cackle and to slander

and just as certainly he was no part of the London literary society of Taylor, Lamb, Reynolds, and the other contributors to the *London Magazine*.

At the depths of his misfortunes in 1823, the Fitzwilliam family offered him a cottage, four miles away from Helpstone at Northborough, and Clare was glad to accept it, because it seemed to promise him security. Clare was grateful to the Fitzwilliams for their kindness, and would not have welcomed the criticisms made of them by later writers. He himself was still part of a society in which the great house was the focus. What Clare failed to realize, however, was the wrench which it would mean to him to move from the cottage where he had spent all his life, the hearth of his native Eden. The move to Northborough is the subject of two of Clare's greatest poems, 'Decay' (pp. 182–4) and 'The Flitting' (pp. 176–82). The first of these poems opens with words which link the two poems together:

> O poesy is on the wane
> For fancys visions all unfitting
> I hardly know her face again
> Nature herself seems on the flitting

Clare is afraid that the springs of his creativeness will have dried up as a consequence of this removal:

> But poesy is passed away
> A withered stalk a naked tree

We have printed 'Decay' and its companion poem, 'The Flitting', in full, so that the reader may appreciate the deracination which Clare felt. Once again, Clare makes it clear in 'The Flitting' that he is speaking of no idealized abstract landscape but of a particular place, by naming Royce Wood, one of his favourite haunts, and the home of his beloved nightingales. Now that he has moved to Northborough it seems to him that:

> The sun een seems to lose its way
> Nor knows the quarter it is in

As he says in 'Decay', when referring to his early days in Helpstone

> I thought the flowers upon the hills
> Were flowers from Adams open gardens,

whereas, after the flitting:

> The stream it is a naked stream
> Where we on sundays used to ramble
> The sky hangs oer a broken dream
> The brambles dwindled to a bramble.

It has sometimes been said that Clare shows no development in his work. These two poems are clear proof of the contrary. If we look at the poems from the 1820 volume (pp. 3–14)—and we must emphasize that we have chosen only the best—they lack the much deeper and more reflective note struck in these great poems of 1832. The latter are poems of Clare's maturity, and though they are full of passion and disillusionment, the passion and disillusionment are contained by the firm thought-structure and accomplished verse of a practised poet. The language is less traditionally poetic than that of such a poem as 'Summer Images' (p. 145), which includes among its splendours the language of Gray and Collins—a language later discarded by Clare for words which came more naturally to him. At the same time, in the poetry of this decade, Clare is still in possession of his faculties, and he has not descended to the restricted range of language and subject-matter of his later asylum lyrics, which have perhaps been overvalued as a whole because of the intensity of one or two.

As a poet, Clare was out of his time. He belongs to the world before the French Revolution, and it must be remembered that times changed more slowly in Helpstone than in London where literary fashion was dictated. Clare could admire Pope when it was the done thing among London literary critics to decry him, or Erasmus Darwin, when Canning and his smart friends had made him ridiculous. The judiciousness of Clare's verdicts on literature is an eighteenth-century judiciousness, founded in good sense and balanced emotion. Although Clare read Keats and Wordsworth and Coleridge, it is not these writers to whom he constantly refers, and it is not the Romantics, apart from Byron, the most eighteenth-century in feeling, who provided him with his early models. This can be illustrated by some of his differences with his publisher. Taylor gave the following advice to Clare:

I have often remarked that your Poetry is much the best when you are not describing common things, and if you would raise your Views generally, & speak of the Appearances of Nature each Month more philosophically (if I may so say) or with more Excitement, you would greatly improve these little poems; some parts of November are extremely good—others are too prosaic—they have too much of the language of common everyday Description;—faithful I grant they are, but that is not all—'What in me is low, Raise & refine' is the way in which you should conceive them as addressing you . . .[1]

When he was in a more impatient mood, he spoke of Clare's first version of 'July' of *The Shepherd's Calendar* as 'a descriptive catalogue in rhyming Prose'. Mrs. Emmerson also joined in with talk to Taylor of Clare proving 'himself capable of higher subjects than talking of Birds & Flowers'.[2] There was a difference of a generation in taste between Taylor and Mrs. Emmerson on one hand and Clare on the other, as well as a difference in quality of judgement. Quite apart from the fact that Clare had no need to inject philosophy and excitement into his poetry, since the excitement was already there for anyone with half an eye, and the only philosophy required was the consistent framework of thought and feeling in which the whole of Clare's work was already shaped, there still remained a gap between London and Helpstone in the 1820s.

Clare's reading had not led him to despise descriptive poetry. The Augustans had a place for it and Clare had a taste for it. Its pace was slower, its conventions were more elaborate than those of the intense Romantic lyric but its origins were perfectly respectable. Cowper, whom Clare admired perhaps above any other poet, had made the descriptive poem a vehicle not only for his observations of nature but for his emotional reactions to it. Clare's emotional reactions to nature are there too, but they are not, except in some very early poems, the reactions of a leisured gentleman but of a working man, and when Taylor occasionally managed to see what Clare's reactions were—to rustic courtship, to magisterial injustice, to middle-class prudery— he preferred to strike them out. Later editors of Clare have shared the post-Romantic enthusiasm for poems of feeling, and so have

[1] Taylor to Clare, 4 March 1826.
[2] Mrs. Emmerson to Clare, 8 December 1826.

tended to discard or to curtail those poems by Clare which do not accord with their picture of him as a Romantic poet. Poems in which he is quietly, even ruminatingly, descriptive, or where he turns to social satire, are set aside as not reflecting his true genius. Yet *The Shepherd's Calendar* is a magnificent example of a sustained descriptive poem in the eighteenth-century tradition. It is based on a month-by-month account of village and farming life, in which human and natural events are very carefully interwoven. The human figures in the landscape are always of importance, and this interest was intended to be strengthened by following each month's descriptive poem by a verse tale related to that month. That is why we have selected from the *Shepherd's Calendar* the poem for February and 'Valentine Eve' which was the verse-tale originally intended to accompany it.

The Parish, which has never been published in full, is a piece of incisive and sustained satire, and by no means disgraces Clare, for its portraits are energetic and its criticisms telling. The informal 'parish council' is neatly pinned to the wall:

> With learning just enough to sign a name
> And skill sufficient parish rates to frame
> And cunning deep enough the poor to cheat
> This learned body for debatings meet...
> Tho many heads the parliment prepare
> And each one claims some wisdom for its share
> Like midnight with her vapours tis so small
> They make but darkness visible with all;

the braggart farmer's son, the fashionable daughter, the hunting curate, the parish clerk make up a set of characters which no satirist need be ashamed of. We can see other village characters in the ballad, 'The Cellar Door' (p. 46), for the alehouse was always one of Clare's favourite places of resort and John Barleycorn one of his best friends. He was not a tea-drinker. If one looks at Hilton's portrait of John Clare as a young man, one can see in an instant what the nineteenth-century Romantics—and for that matter, their descendants in the twentieth century—would like Clare to have been. The portrait is one of those generic portraits of Keats, Shelley, Byron, Rupert Brooke, or who-you-will, that might be interchanged without anyone being much concerned about the differences. The poet is handsome by right, curly-haired and rather fey, but beautifully wholesome in the carefully arranged disorder of his clothes. The same prettification was carried out by Hilton on Clare's cottage, so that the poet was obliged to remark that Hilton 'has forced poor J. C. from his flail & spade to strut on canvas in the town of humour . . . I will take him from his "water nymphs" to lye on the hobs of our dirty cottages to be read by every greazy thumbed wench & chubby clown'.[1]

Clare was never what his critics would like him to have been. He was at one and the same time coarser and more delicate of sentiment than they thought, fonder of his beer and a pretty ankle than they wanted to admit, yet more deeply honourable and responsible than they could imagine, more accurate in his observation than they could judge and more reflective than they could perceive. As a poet he was certainly much more varied in his forms of expression than the usual anthology selected from his poems would suggest.

None of his talents saved him during his lifetime from almost total oblivion. *The Shepherd's Calendar* sold very badly, and Clare was obliged to attempt the publication of *The Midsummer Cushion* by obtaining subscriptions. Although he was still hopeful of success, his increasing ill health forced him to abandon the project, and finally *The Rural Muse* was published in 1835 by How and Whittaker. The beautifully transcribed manuscript of *The Midsummer Cushion* is still preserved by Peterborough Museum Society, and is a monument to Clare's frustrations and failure. We have included in this selection several poems from it (pp. 33–184, *passim*). It is particularly rich in sonnets, a verse-form with which Clare had great success. The sonnets are the pen-and-ink sketches of the great painter—they capture the scene just as the artist saw it before he had time to reflect deeply upon it. Just as the artist's sketches sometimes form the basis of a more finished canvas, so Clare's sonnets were sometimes worked upon to make longer poems, but mostly they exist solely for themselves, and their appeal lies in their freshness. They portray birds and their nests, animals, seasons, times of day, and rural labours and re-creations. They lie so rich and profuse among his work that it is very difficult to choose from them, and like a child sorting sea-shells in a bucket, one finds it almost impossible to throw one away. It is possible that they also represent for Clare a kind of self-discipline, forcing him to concentrate and obtain his effects with economy, where in other poems he allowed himself to wander a little aimlessly and in

[1] Clare to Taylor, 20 May 1820.

a more expansive mood. The measure of his success can be judged by the way in which he arrests the reader's attention with his first lines:

> 'Winter is come in earnest . . .'
> 'I love at eventide to walk alone'
> 'The autumn morning waked by many a gun'
> 'Hugh Elm thy rifted trunk all notched and scarred'
> 'I had a joy and keep it still alive'.

The discipline, however, is sometimes relaxed by his habit of writing two or three sonnets in a sequence as in 'The Flood' (p. 144), 'Signs of Winter' (p. 142), and 'The Badger' (p. 84). One would not expect, and generally does not find, any great weight of thoughts in the sonnets, but they are a series of images, and Clare's images are very evocative. The two sonnets 'Early Images' (p. 152) illustrate this very clearly, where the images of early morning are threaded together like beads on a string. Many of these sonnets found their way into newspapers, and though Clare was seldom paid for their publication, they reached a public which might otherwise have never seen them at all.

The failure to publish *The Midsummer Cushion* and the poor response by the public to *The Rural Muse*, which partly replaced it, meant the end of the road for Clare's ambitions. He had been badly disturbed, now and again, by the 'blue devils' for several years before he entered Matthew Allen's private asylum in Epping Forest, as a voluntary patient, in 1837. He was well treated at High Beech, allowed a considerable amount of freedom, and encouraged to write poetry, but in his disturbed frame of mind he was quite unable to understand why he was separated from Helpstone and his family. He suffered delusions, believing himself at different times to be Ben Caunt, a well-known prizefighter, Lord Byron, Robert Burns, and various other people. To his delusion that he was Byron, whose rebellious personality had always fascinated Clare and whose funeral he had witnessed in London, we owe two poems, 'Child Harold' and 'Don Juan',[1] which were begun at High Beech. The first of these poems is a very interesting performance. It is a long poem of nine-line stanzas, interspersed with lyrical poems which explore or intensify the emotions established in the narrative stanzas. It has some

---

[1] For the full text of these poems, see *Later Poems of John Clare*, ed. E. Robinson and G. Summerfield, Manchester, 1964.

of the characteristics of Byron's verse, but it is an attempt by Clare, even in his madness, to get to grips with reality, to ascertain his own personality, and to resolve the conflict between vision and reality. One of his dilemmas in it is to make up his mind about Mary. 'How is it possible', he seems to be asking, 'that Mary, the archetype of innocence and freshness, should abandon me?' Mary's failure to stand by him appears to reflect the hypocrisy and double-dealing of the whole of society, and Clare imagines that it is his own truthfulness which has caused society to turn upon him and to imprison him. The poem moves from intensely detailed personal circumstances to moments of generalization, and at its best attains a glowing quality not unlike that of a Samuel Palmer painting:

> The Paigles Bloom In Showers In Grassy Close
> How Sweet To Be Among Their Blossoms Led
> And Hear Sweet Nature To Herself Discourse
> While Pale The Moon Is Bering Over Head
> And Hear The Grazeing Cattle Softly Tread
> Cropping The Hedgerows Newly Leafing Thorn
> Sounds Soft As Visions Murmured Oer In Bed
> At Dusky Eve or Sober Silent Morn
> For such Delights Twere Happy Man Was Born

The capitalization of the letters is a sympton of Clare's madness, but the verse itself is entirely lucid in such moments as these, and indeed there is a kind of sense even in the most troubled sections of the poem. 'Child Harold' is a haunting poem and shows Clare still struggling, even in a madhouse, to make sense of his tragic existence.

Clare ran away from High Beech in 1841 and walked the whole way back to Northamptonshire to rejoin Mary, who, he thought, was waiting for him and to whom he had been writing while he was in the asylum. A few miles from his home he was collected in a wagon by Patty and taken back to their cottage. On his return he wrote an account of his escape, the 'Journey out of Essex' (pp. 184-91), which tells of his adventures and the hardships he endured. Though he had come home to Northamptonshire, it was all to no avail, and a few months later he was certified insane by Dr. Fenwick Skrimshire and sent to the Northampton General Asylum, where he spent his days until death in May 1864. We might expect the date of this second committal to an asylum, especially when it was to last the rest of his life, to be the end of Clare as a poet. Even here, however, Clare defies prediction. Hundreds of his poems survive from his years at Northampton, and many more may have been lost. Clare's life at Northampton contrasts with the frightening account of madness in *Jane Eyre*. The building where Clare was kept is still standing and is now a private mental hospital. It is a gracious building with lofty rooms, and elegant doors and plastered ceilings, with most beautiful private grounds at the rear of the building. Clare was allowed a good deal of freedom, often walked into the town and was a familiar figure to the townspeople sitting in the porch of All Saints' Church. The House Steward of the Asylum, W. F. Knight, was a sensitive man, interested in literature, who gave his friendship to Clare and encouraged him to write, and it is through his interest that so many of Clare's poems written at this time survive, for Knight himself transcribed many of them into two large volumes which are now in Northampton Public Library. Some of the poems are addressed to girls whom Clare met in Northampton, in shops or in ale-houses, as he strolled about the town. Their freshness and youth evoked for him the joys of his early life and of his association with Mary, and it is fitting that these otherwise obscure young friends of his should gain an immortality in his poetry.

Though most of the poems written in his closing years are love songs or ballads, and though most of them, at least superficially, speak of enjoyments in nature, felt in the past or even in the present, a sombre note is occasionally struck. The consequence of free will in Adam's Paradise was the Fall and the introduction of sin into the world. Thus the time would come when there would be a terrible Day of Judgement. The sequence is followed in 'Spring' in Thomson's *Seasons*: first a picture of Eden, showing the contentment of rural society, enjoying cheerful labour and refreshed by song; then the Fall where all the harmony of Eden is destroyed; and then the Deluge and the Day of Judgement. In Clare's poetry, the theme of Judgement, which had always been there, grew stronger and gained fuller expression in his later years. In 1841 he wrote the apocalyptic poem:

> There is a day a dreadful day
> Still following the past
> When sun and moon are past away
> And mingle with the blast

There is a vision in my eye
A vacuum oer my mind
Sometimes as on the sea I lye
Mid roaring waves and wind

Imitations of the psalms often follow a similar trend, and thunder and shipwreck are frequent subjects. His early reading of Falconer's *Shipwreck* and similar works now provided him with an imagery of terror. 'An invite to Eternity' (p. 196) asks the maiden to go with the poet:

Where the path hath lost its way
Where the sun forgets the day

and

Where stones will turn to flooding streams
Where plains will rise like ocean waves
Where life will fade like visioned dreams
And mountains darken into caves

Even the poems which ostensibly deal with lighter matters like the poem about the ladybird or 'Clock a Clay' (p. 199) may have a disturbing note of fear and insecurity about them, while the famous 'I am' (p. 195) speaks of 'the living sea of waking dreams'. There is no question that Clare in his later years developed a very distinctive voice, an unmistakable intensity and vibrance, such as the later pictures by Van Gogh possess, but we must also guard against attributing too much importance to the poems of his madness because we live in an age fascinated by the problems of mental stress. It is salutary, after reading some of the last poems, to turn back to a poem like 'Sabbath Bells' (p. 157) where the free response of Clare to Nature is untinged by despair and doubt or to the Augustan calm of 'Summer Images' (p. 145) or 'The Nightingales Nest' (p. 73). And when one does so, it is the continuity of Clare's life and ways of thought and feeling which claims one's attention, rather than the disruptions of insanity.

Finally it ought to be remembered that Clare would still have been one of the finest poets of his century if he had died in 1837 before he had entered an asylum. His published work at that time was already a considerable achievement, even though it had been tampered with by Taylor. And even in 1837 there were many poems still in manuscript which had never been published and none of Clare's prose had been published at all. He was a most prolific and fertile writer, and could perhaps be called 'the green man of English poetry'. His work is still read a hundred years after his death and his fame will grow when his work is presented in a form which will make some overall estimate of it possible. Clare asked for no pretentious gravestone. He felt that if his work lived, then an imposing tombstone would be unnecessary; if his work did not live, then no tombstone, however elaborate, would save him from oblivion. There is no doubt that Clare will live.

1792 Shelley born.

1793 John Clare born at Helpstone, Northants., 13 July.

1794 Blake's *Songs of Experience*. Erasmus Darwin's *Zoönomia*.

1795 Keats born. Speenhamland.

1796 Death of Burns.

1797 Bewick's *History of British Birds*.

1798 Battle of the Nile. *Lyrical Ballads*. Cowper: *On the Receipt of my Mother's Picture*.

1799 Religious Tract Society founded.

1800 Bloomfield's *The Farmer's Boy*. Death of Cowper.

1802 Scott's *Minstrelsy of the Scottish Border*. Bloomfield's *Rural Tales*.

1803 Hayley's *Life of Cowper*.

1804 Napoleon proclaimed Emperor.

1805 Cary's translation of Dante's *Inferno*. Battle of Trafalgar (21 October).

1806 Roscoe's *The Butterfly's Ball and Grasshopper's Feast*; Byron's *Fugitive Pieces*.

1807 Kirke White's *Remains*.

1808 Byron sails for the Mediterranean.

1809 Battle of Corunna; Enclosure Act for Helpstone.

1810 Crabbe's *The Borough*.

1811 Luddite Riots. Bloomfield's *The Banks of the Wye*.

1812 Byron's *Childe Harold* (I and II).

1813 Coleridge's *Remorse*.

1814 Cary completes his translation of Dante's *Divina Commedia*.

1815 Waterloo: Napoleon exiled to St. Helena. Byron's *Hebrew Melodies*.

1816 Shelley's *Alastor*.

1817 Keats's *Poems*.

1818 Keats's *Endymion*.

1820   Publication of *Poems Descriptive of Rural Life and Scenery*. Marriage to Martha Turner.

1821   *Poems Descriptive*, Fourth Edition. *The Village Minstrel and other Poems*. Taylor acquires the *London Magazine*. Death of Keats.

1822   Death of Shelley.

1823   Death of Octavius Gilchrist. Elizabeth Kent's *Flora Domestica*.

1824   Death of Byron. First number of Alaric Watts's *Literary Souvenir*. Taylor withdraws from the *London Magazine*.

1825   Cunningham's *Songs of Scotland, Ancient and Modern*. Death of Lord Radstock. Taylor and Hessey dissolve their partnership.

1826   Hone's *Every Day Book*.

1827   Publication of *The Shepherd's Calendar, with Village Stories and Other Poems*.

1828   Lockhart's *Life of Burns*.

1829   Hogg's *The Shepherd's Calendar*; Tennyson's *Timbuctoo*.

1830   Publication of Dr. Matthew Allen's *Cases of Insanity*. Moore's *Life of Byron*. Captain Swing Riots.

1831   Ebenezer Elliott's *Corn-Law Rhymes*.

1832   Clare leaves Helpstone and moves to Northborough. Reform Act.

1834   Poor Law Reform Act.

1835   Publication of *The Rural Muse*.

1837   Publication of Dr. Matthew Allen's *Classification of the Insane*; Clare removed to High Beech, Epping. Accession of Queen Victoria.

1841   Clare escapes from High Beech (July) and is removed to Northampton (December).

1845   W. F. Knight appointed House Steward, Northampton Asylum.

1849   Death of Thomas Inskip, and of Peter De Wint.

1850   W. F. Knight leaves Northampton for Birmingham.

1864   Clare dies at Northampton, May 20th. John Taylor dies.

1865   W. B. Yeats born.

SELECT BIBLIOGRAPHY

The recent editions of the poetry

Geoffrey Grigson (ed.): *Poems of John Clare's Madness* (London, 1949).

> Textually a very unreliable volume; but it contains a most illuminating Introduction.

Geoffrey Grigson (ed.): *Selected Poems* (Muses' Library, 1950).

> Approximately a third of the text draws on the unreliable readings of *Poems of John Clare's Madness*.

J. W. Tibble (ed.): *The Poems of John Clare* (London, 1935).

> A fairly comprehensive *selection* of Clare's poetry; textually, an amalgam of earlier, improved, editions and manuscript sources; inadequately annotated and very far from a definitive edition.

J. W. and A. Tibble (edd.): *Selected Poems* (Everyman, 1965).

> An unsatisfactory volume which reprints Taylor's truncated text of *The Shepherd's Calendar* and which is editorially inconsistent in its handling of the text of the later poems.

Eric Robinson and Geoffrey Summerfield (edd.): *The Later Poems* (Manchester, 1964).

> An attempt to present Clare's work of the asylum years in the form in which he wrote it.

Eric Robinson and Geoffrey Summerfield (edd.): *The Shepherd's Calendar* (Oxford, 1964).

> A reclamation of Clare's most ambitious single poem from the available MS. sources.

Biographical

Frederick W. Martin: *The Life of John Clare*, 2nd edn., with an Introduction and Notes by Eric Robinson and Geoffrey Summerfield (London, 1964).

> This remains the freshest and most illuminating of the biographies.

J. L. Cherry: *Life and Remains of John Clare* (London and Northampton, 1873).

> An indifferent biography, but the volume is interesting for its 220 pages of Clare's later poetry and prose, even though the text is bowdlerized.

Edmund Blunden (ed.): *Sketches in the Life of John Clare* (London, 1931).

A well edited selection from the mass of Clare's autobiographical notes.

Edmund Blunden: *Keats's Publisher, A Memoir of John Taylor* (London, 1936).

An interesting and lucid account of Clare's publisher, but rather over-generous in its appraisal of Taylor's treatment of his authors.

J. W. and A. Tibble: *John Clare, A Life* (London, 1932).

A comprehensive, detailed biography, now superseded in matters of detail by the same authors' *John Clare: His Life and Poetry* (London, 1956).

Critical and textual

Edward Thomas: *Feminine Influence on the Poets* (London, n.d.).

John Middleton Murry: *John Clare and Other Studies* (London, 1950).

John Middleton Murry: *Unprofessional Essays* (London, 1956).

Kenneth Richmond: *Poetry and the People* (London, 1947).

C. Day Lewis: *The Lyric Impulse* (London, 1965).

Robert Graves: *The Crowning Privilege* (Penguin, 1959).

Anne Elizabeth Baker: *Glossary of Northamptonshire Words and Phrases* (London and Northampton, 1854, 2 vols.).

A comprehensive and detailed attempt to cope with the riches of Clare's dialect, based in part on a reading of Clare's poetry and on interviews with him in the Asylum at Northampton.

NOTE ON THE TEXT

THE text is everywhere taken from the original manuscripts but the full editorial apparatus is reserved for our projected edition of Clare's poetry in the Oxford English Text Series. For the few early poems, first published in 1820, the existing manuscripts are heavily corrected for spelling and punctuation, sometimes by Clare, presumably on someone else's advice, or by another hand, and do not seem to be the manuscripts from which the published text was prepared. Accordingly in these poems, and in 'Autumn', we have supplemented the manuscripts by printing lines from the first edition and enclosing them in square brackets [   ]. We have also used square brackets for letters and words omitted by Clare.

Where a dialect word or a confusing misspelling occurs we have referred the reader to the Glossary by an asterisk* but this is done only when the word occurs for the first time in this volume, in order to avoid littering the text. When in doubt the reader is advised to consult the Glossary. We also give a special warning about Clare's habit of omitting the apostrophe in such phrases as: I'm, we'll, they'll, etc.

Prose passages have been left unpunctuated, but, to assist the reader, a gap is left between sentences. In the list of contents it will be observed that the titles of prose passages have been indented.

Dedication to ****

O M *** thou that once made all
What youthful dreams coud pleasure call
That once did love to walk with me
And own thy taste for scenery
That sat for hours by wood and brook
And stopt thy curious flowers to look
Were all that met thy artless gaze
Enjoyd thy smiles and won thy praise
O thou that did sincerely love
The cuckoos note and cooing dove
And stood in raptures oft to hear
The blackbirds music wild and clear
That chasd sleep from thy lovly eyes
To see the morning lark arise
And made thy evening rambles long
To list the crickets chittering* song
Thou that on sabbath noons sought bowers
To read away the sultry hours
Were roseys hung the cool to share
With thee a blossom full as fair
Oft withering from noons scorching look
And fluttering dropping on thy book
Wispering morals as they fell
What thou ere this hath provd too well
Picturing stories sad and true
Beneath thy bright eyes beaming blue
How youth and beauty fades and dyes
The sweetest has the least to prize
How blissfull pleasures fade away
That have the shortest time to stay
As suns that blest thy eyes and mine
Are but alowd a day to shine
And fairest days without a cloud
A gloomy evening waits to shroud

So spoke the fading dropping flowers
That perishd in thy musing hours
I know not wether thou descryd
But I coud hear them by thy side
But thy warm heart tho easy wrung
Woud not be mellancholy long
If such was felt the cheering day
Woud quickly chase their glooms away
For thou sought fancys sweet to look
In every hour and every nook
To thee earth swarmd with lovly things
The butterflye with spangld wings
And dragon flye and humble bee
Hummd dreams of paradise to thee
And o thou fairest dearest still
If natures wild mysterious skill
Beams that same rapture in thine eye
And left a love that cannot dye
If that fond taste was born to last
Nor vanishd with the summers past
If seasons as they usd to be
Still meet a favourd smile with thee
Then thou accept for memorys sake
All I can give or thou canst take
A parted record known to thee
Of what has been no more to be
The pleasant past the future sorrow
The blest today and sad tomorrow—
Descriptions wild of summer walks
By hedges lanes and trackless balks
And many an old familiar scene
Were thou has oft my partner been
Were thou enrapt in wild delight
Hast lingerd morning noon and night
And were to fancys rapturd thrill
Thy lovly memory lingers still
Thy flowers still bloom and look the while
As tho they witnessd marys smile
The birds still sing thy favourd lays

2

As tho they sung for marys praise
And bees hum glad and fearless bye
As tho their tender friend was nigh
O if with thee those raptures live
Accept the trifle which I give
Tho lost to pleasures witnessd then
Tho parted neer to meet agen
My aching heart is surely free
To dedicate its thoughts to thee
Then thou accept and if a smile
Lights on the page thou reads the while
If aught bespeaks those banishd hours
Of beauty in thy favourd flowers
Or scenes recall of happy days
That claims as wont thy ready praise
Tho I so long have lost the claim
To joys which wear thy gentle name
Tho thy sweet face so long unseen
Seems types of charms that neer hath been
Thy voice so long in silence bound
To me that I forget the sound
And tho thy presence warms my theme
Like beauty floating in a dream
Yet I will think that such may be
Tho buried secrets all to me
And if it be as hopes portray
Then will thy smiles like dews of heaven
Cheer my lone walks my toils repay
And all I ask be given

Noon

ALL how silent and how still,
Nothing heard but yonder mill;
While the dazzled eye surveys
All around a liquid blaze;
And amid the scorching gleams,
If we earnest look it seems

3

As if crooked bits of glass
Seem'd repeatedly to pass.
O! for a puffing breeze to blow,
But breezes all are strangers now.
Not a twig is seen to shake,
Nor the smallest bent* to quake;
From the river's muddy side,
Not a curve is seen to glide;
And no longer in the stream,
Watching lies the silver bream,
Forcing from repeated springs,
'Verges in successive rings.'

Bees are faint and cease to hum,
Birds are overpow'r'd and dumb;
And no more love's oaten strains,
Sweetly through the air complains;
Rural voices all are mute;
Tuneless lies the pipe and flute;
Shepherds with their panting sheep,
In the swaliest* corner creep; ·
And from the tormenting heat,
All are wishing to retreat;
Huddled up in grass and flow'rs,
Mowers wait for cooler hours;
And the cow-boy seeks the sedge,
Ramping* in the woodland hedge,
While his cattle o'er the vales,
Scamper with uplifted tails;
Others not so wild and mad,
That can better bear the gad,
Underneath the hedge-row lunge*
Or, if nigh, in waters plunge;

    O to see how flow'rs are took!
How it grieves me when I look:—
Ragged-robbins once so pink
Now are turn'd as black as ink,

And their leaves being scorch'd so much
Even crumble at the touch.
Drowking* lies the meadow-sweet
Flopping down beneath one's feet;
While to all the flow'rs that blow,
If in open air they grow,
Th'injurious deed alike is done
By the hot relentless sun.
E'en the dew is parched up
From the teazle's jointed cup.—
O poor birds where must ye fly,
Now your water-pots are dry?
If ye stay upon the heath
Ye'll be chok'd and clamm'd* to death
Therefore leave the shadeless goss,*
Seek the spring-head lin'd with moss

There your little feet may stand,
Safely printing on the sand;
While in full possession, where
Purling eddies ripple clear,
You with ease and plenty blest,
Sip the coolest and the best;
Then away and wet your throats,
Cheer me with your warbling notes;
'Twill hot Noon the more revive:
While I wander to contrive
For myself a place as good,
In the middle of a wood;
There, aside some mossy bank,
Where the grass in bunches rank
Lifts its down on spindles high,
Shall be where I'll choose to lie;
Fearless of the things that creep,
There I'll think and there I'll sleep;
Caring not to stir at all,
Till the dew begins to fall.

5

What is Life?

AND what is Life? an hour-glass on the run
A mist retreating from the morning sun
   A busy bustling still repeated dream
Its length? A moment's pause, a moment's thought
   And happiness? A bubble on the stream
That in the act of siezing shrinks to nought

Vain hopes—what are they? Puffing gales of morn
That of its charms divests the dewy lawn
   And robs each flowret of its gem and dies
A cobweb hiding disappointments thorn
   Which stings more keenly thro' the thin disguise

And thou, O trouble? Nothing can suppose,
And sure the Power of Wisdom only knows,
   What need requireth thee.
So free and lib'ral as thy bounty flows,
   Some necessary cause must surely be.

And what is death? Is still the cause unfound
The dark mysterious name of horrid sound
   A long and ling'ring sleep the weary crave—
And peace—where can its happiness abound?
   No where at all but Heaven and the grave

Then what is Life? When stript of its disguise
   A thing to be desir'd it cannot be
Since every thing that meets our foolish eyes
   Gives proof sufficient of its vanity
'Tis but a trial all must undergo
   To teach unthankful mortals how to prize
That happiness vain man's denied to know
   Untill he's call'd to claim it in the skies.

6

The Harvest Morning

COCKS wake the early morn with many a crow
Loud ticking village clock has counted four
The labouring rustic hears his restless foe
And weary bones and pains complaining sore
Hobbles to fetch his horses from the moor
While some are left to teem* the loaded corn
Which night unfinished left agen the door
And bird boy scaring sounds his hollow horn
What busy bustling labouring scene[s] now mark the harvest
   morn

Swift hies the waggon in the field to load
And wakes the early morn wi rattling sound
And hogs and geese now throng the dusty road
Grunting and gabbling in contention round
The barley ears that litter on the ground
What printing traces mark the waggons way
[What dusty bustling wakens echo round;
How drive the sun's warm beams the mist away;
How labour sweats and toils, and dreads the sultry day!]

The mower scythe now oer his shoulder leans
And wetting* jars a sharp shill* tinkling sound
Then swaps again mong corn and rustling beans
And swath by swath flops lengthening oer the ground
[While 'neath some friendly heap, snug shelter'd round
From spoiling sun, lies hid the heart's delight;
And hearty soaks oft hand the bottle round,
Their toils pursuing with redoubled might—
Great praise to him be due that brought its birth to light.

Upon the waggon now, with eager bound,
The lusty picker whirls the rustling sheaves;
Or, resting ponderous creaking fork aground,
Boastful at once whole shocks of barley heaves:
The loading boy revengeful inly grieves

7

To find his unmatch'd strength and power decay;
The barley horn his garments interweaves;
Smarting and sweating 'neath the sultry day,
With muttering curses stung, he mauls the heaps away.

A motley group the clearing field surround:
Sons of Humanity, oh ne'er deny
The humble gleaner entrance in your ground;
Winter's sad cold, and Poverty are nigh.
Grudge not from Providence the scant supply:
You'll never miss it from your ample store.
Who gives denial,—harden'd, hungry hound,—
May never blessings crowd his hated door!
But he shall never lack, that giveth to the poor.

Ah, lovely Emma! mingling with the rest,
Thy beauties blooming in low life unseen,
Thy rosy cheeks, thy sweetly swelling breast;
But ill it suits thee in the stubs to glean.
O Poverty! how basely you demean
The imprison'd worth your rigid fates confine;
Not fancied charms of an Arcadian queen,
So sweet as Emma's real beauties shine:
Had Fortune blest, sweet girl, this lot had ne'er been thine.

The sun's increasing heat now mounted high,
Refreshment must recruit exhausted power;
The waggon stops, the busy tool's thrown by,
And 'neath a shock's enjoy'd the bevering hour.*
The bashful maid, sweet health's engaging flower,
Lingering behind, o'er rake still blushing bends;
And when to take the horn fond swains implore,
With feign'd excuses its dislike pretends.
So pass the bevering hours, so Harvest Morning ends.

O Rural Life! what charms thy meanness hide;
What sweet descriptions bards disdain to sing;

What loves, what graces on thy plains abide:
Oh, could I soar me on the Muse's wing,
What rifled charms should my researches bring!
Pleas'd would I wander where these charms reside;
Of rural sports and beauties would I sing;
Those beauties, Wealth, which you in vain deride,
Beauties of richest bloom, superior to your pride.]

I ALWAYS feel delighted when an object in nature brings up in ones mind an image of poetry that describes it from some favourite Author   you have a better oppertunity of consulting books then I have   therefore I will set down a list of favourite Poems and Poets who went to nature for their images so that you may consult them and share the feelings and pleasures which I describe   your favourite Chaucer is one   Passages in Spencer Cowleys Grasshopper and Swallow Passages in Shakspear Miltons Allegro and Penseroso and Parts of Comus the Elizabethian Poets of glorious memory Gays Shepherds week Greens Spleen Thompsons Seasons Collins Ode to Evening Dyers Grongar hill and Fleece Shenstones Schoolmistress Greys Ode to Spring T. Wartons April Summer Hamlet and Ode to a friend Cowpers Task Wordsworth Logans Ode to the Cuckoo Langhorns Fables of Flora Jagos Blackbirds Bloomfields Witchwood Forest Shooters hill etc with Hurdis's Evening Walk in the village Curate and many others that may have slipt my memry . . . the man of taste . . . never sees the daisey without thinking of Burns and who sees the taller buttercup carpeting the closes in golden fringe without a remembrance of Chattertons beautiful mention of it . . . 'The kingcup brasted with the morning dew'   other flowers crowd my imagination with their poetic assosiations but I have no room for them   the clown knows nothing of these pleasures   he knows they are flowers and just turns an eye on them and plods bye   therefore as I said before to look on nature with a poetic eye magnifys the pleasure she herself being the very essence and soul of Poesy

(from a letter to Messrs. Taylor and Hessey, 1822)

Summer Evening

THE sinken sun is takin leave
And sweetly gilds the edge of eve
While purple [clouds] of deepening dye
Huddling hang the western skye
Crows crowd quaking* over head
Hastening to the woods to bed
Cooing sits the lonly dove
Calling home her abscent love
Kirchip kirchip mong the wheat
Partridge distant partridge greet
Beckening call to those that roam
Guiding the squandering covey home
Swallows check their rambling flight
And twittering on the chimney light
Round the pond the martins flirt
Their snowy breasts bedawbd in dirt
While the mason neath the slates
Each morter bearing bird awaits
Untaught by art each labouring spouse
Curious daubs his hanging house
Bats flit by in hood and cowl
Thro the barn hole pops the owl
From the hedge the beetles boom
Heedless buz and drousy hum
Haunting every bushy place
Flopping in the labourers face
Now the snail has made his ring
And the moth with snowy wing
Fluttring plays from bent to bent
Bending down with dews besprent
Then on resting branches hing*
Stren[g]th to ferry oer the spring
From the haycocks moistend heaps
Frogs now take their vaunting leaps
And along the shaven mead
Quickly travelling the[y] proceed
Flying from their speckled sides

Dewdrops bounce as grass divides
[Now the blue fog creeps along,
And the bird's forgot his song:]
Flowrets sleep within their hoods
Daisys button into buds
From soiling dew the butter cup
Shuts his golden jewels up
And the Rose and woodbine they
Wait again the smiles of day
Neath the willows wavy boughs
Nelly singing milks her cows
While the streamlet bubling bye
Joins in murmuring melody

Now the hedger hides his bill
And with his faggot climbs the hill
Driver Giles wi rumbling joll*
And blind ball* jostles home the roll
Whilom Ralph for doll* to wait
Lolls him oer the pasture gate
Swains to fold their sheep begin
Dogs bark loud to drive em in
Plough men from their furrowy seams
Loose the weary fainting team
Ball wi cirging* lashes weald
Still so slow to drive afield
Eager blundering from the plough
Wants no wip to drive him now
At the stable door he stands
Looking round for friendly hands
To loose the door its fastening pin
Ungear him now and let him in
Round the Yard a thousand ways
The beest in expectation gaze
Tugging at the loads of hay
As passing fotherers* hugs away
And hogs wi grumbling deafening noise
Bother round the server boys

And all around a motly troop
Anxious claim their suppering up
From the rest a blest release
Gabbling goes the fighting geese
Waddling homward to their bed
In their warm straw litterd shed
Nighted by unseen delay
Poking hens then loose* their way
Crafty cats now sit to watch
Sparrows fighting on the thatch
Dogs lick their lips and wag their tails
When doll brings in the milking pails
With stroaks and pats their welcomd in
And they with looking thanks begin
She dips the milk pail brimming oer
And hides the dish behind the door

    Prone to mischief boys are met
Gen the heaves* the ladders set
Sly they climb and softly tread
To catch the sparrow on his bed
And kill em O in cruel pride
Knocking gen the ladderside
Cursd barbarians pass me by
Come not turks my cottage nigh
Sure my sparrows are my own
Let ye then my birds alone
Sparrows come from foes severe
Fearless come yere welcome here
My heart yearns for fates like thine
A sparrows lifes as sweet as mine
To my cottage then resort
Much I love your chirping note
Wi my own hands to form a nest
Ill gi ye shelter peace and rest
Trifling are the deed[s] ye do
Grait the pains ye undergo
Cruel man woud Justice serve
Their crueltys as they deserve

And justest punishment pursue
And do as they to others do
Ye mourning chirpers fluttering here
They woud no doubt be less severe
{Tho ye pluck the farmers wheat} [1]
{Hunger forces all to eat   }
Foolhardy clown neer grudge the wheat
Which hunger forces them to eat
Your blinded eyes worst foes to you
Neer see the good which sparrows do
Did not the sparrows watching round
Pick up the insect from your grounds
Did not they tend your rising grain
You vain might sow—to reap in vain
Thus providence when understood
Her end and aim is doing good
Sends nothing here without its use
Which Ignorance loads with its abuse
Thus fools despise the blessing sent
And mocks the givers good intent
O god let me the best pursue
As Id have other do to me
Let me the same to others do
And learn at least Humanity

   Dark and darker glooms the sky
Sleep gins close the labourers eye
Dobson on his greensward seat
Where neighbours often neighbour meet
Of c[r]ops to talk and work in hand
And battle News from foreign land
His last wift* hes puffing out
And Judie putting to the rout
Who gossiping takes great delight
To shool* her nitting out at night
Jingling newsing bout the town
Spite o dobs disliking frown

[1] Alternative lines in MS.

Chattering at her neighbours door
The summons warn her to give oer
[Prepar'd to start, she soodles* home,
Her knitting twirling o'er her thumb
As, loth to leave, afraid to stay,
She bawls her story all the way:
The tale so fraught with 'ticing charms,
Her apron folded o'er her arms,
She leaves the unfinished tale, in pain.
To end as evening comes again;
And in the cottage gangs* with dread,
To meet old Dobson's timely frown,
Who grumbling sits, prepar'd for bed,
While she stands chelping* 'bout the town.]

   Night winds now on sutty wings
In the cotters chimney sings
Sweet I raise my drowsy head
Thoughtful stretching on my bed
Listning to the ushering charms
That shakes the Elm trees mossy arms
Till soft slumbers stronger creep
Then rocked by winds I fall to sleep

Part of *Childhood* or *The Past*

THE past it is a magic word
Too beautiful to last
It looks back like a lovely face
Who can forget the past
Theres music in its childhood
Thats known in every tongue
Like the music of the wildwood
All chorus to the song

The happy dream the joyous play
The life without a sigh
The beauty thoughts can neer pourtray
In those four letters lye

The painters beauty breathing art
The poets speaking pens
Can neer call back a thousand part
Of what that word contains

. . . . .

Youth revels at its rising hour
With more then* summer joys
And rapture holds the fairey flower
Which reason soon destroys
O sweet the bliss which fancy feigns
To hide the eyes of truth
And beautious still the charm appears
Of faces loved in youth

And spring returns the blooming year
Just as it used to be
And joys in youthful smiles appear
To mock the change in me
Each sight leaves memory ill at ease
And stirs an aching bosom
To think that seasons sweet as these
With me are out of blossom

The finest summer sinks in shade
The sweetest blossom dies
And age finds every beauty fade
That youth esteemed a prize
The play breaks up the blossom dies
And childhood dissapears
For higher dooms ambition tries
And care grows into years

But time we often blame him wrong
That rude destroying time
And follow him with sorrows song
When he hath done no crime
Our joys in youth are often sold
In follys thoughtless fray

And many feel their hearts grow old
Before their heads are grey

The past there lies in that one word
Joys more then wealth can crown
Nor could a million call them back
Though muses wrote them down
The sweetest joys imagined yet
The beautys that surpast
The dearest joys man ever met
Are all among the past

Sport in the Meadows

MAY time is to the meadows coming in
And cowslap* peeps have gotten eer so big
And water blabs* and all their golden kin
Crowd round the shallows by the striding brig
Daisys and buttercups and lady smocks
Are all abouten shining here and there
Nodding about their gold and yellow locks
Like morts of folken flocking at a fair
The sheep and cows are crowding for a share
And snatch the blossoms in such eager haste
That basket bearing childern running there
Do think within their hearts theyll get them all
And hoot and drive them from their graceless waste
As though there wan't a cowslap peep to spare
For they want some for tea and some for wine
And some to maken up a cucka ball*
To throw accross the garlands silken line
That reaches oer the street from wall to wall
Good gracious me how merrily they fare
One sees a fairer cowslap then the rest
And off they shout—the foremost bidding fair
To get the prize—and earnest half and jest
The next one pops her down—and from her hand
Her basket falls and out her cowslaps all

Tumble and litter there—the merry band
In laughing friendship round about her fall
To helpen gather up the littered flowers
That she no loss may mourn—and now the wind
In frolic mood among the merry hours
Wakens with sudden start and tosses off
Some untied bonnet on its dancing wings
Away they follow with a scream and laugh
And aye the youngest ever lags behind
Till on the deep lakes very brink it hings
They shout and catch it and away they start
The chace for cowslaps merry as before
And each one seems so anxious at the heart
As they would even get them all and more
One climbs a molehill for a bunch of may
One stands on tiptoe for a linnets nest
And pricks her hand and throws her flowers away
And runs for plantain leaves to have it drest
So do they run abouten all the day
And teaze the grass hid larks from getting rest
—Scarce give they time in their unruley haste
To tie a shoestring that the grass unties
And thus they run the meadows bloom to waste
Till even comes and dulls their phantasys
When one finds losses out to stifle smiles
Of silken bonnet strings—and uthers sigh
Oer garments rent in clambering over stiles
Yet in the morning fresh afield they hie
Bidding the last days troubles a good bye
When red pied cow again their coming hears
And ere they clap the gate she tosses up
Her head and hastens from the sport she fears
The old yoe* calls her lamb nor cares to stoop
To crop a cowslap in their company
Thus merrily the little noisey troop
Along the grass as rude marauders hie
For ever noisey and forever gay
While keeping in the meadow holiday

I NEVER had much relish for the pastimes of youth   instead of going out on the green at the town end on Winter sundays to play football I stuck to my corner stool poreing over a book   in fact I grew so fond of being alone at last that my mother was feign to force me into company for the neighbours had assured her mind into the fact that I was no better then crazy.

I usd to be very fond of fishing and of a sunday morning I have been out before the sun delving for worms in some old weed blanketed dunghill and steering off across the wet grain* that overhung the narrow path and then I used to stoop to wring my wet trouser bottoms now and then and off agen beating the heavy drops off the grain with my pole end   I usd also to be very fond of poking about the hedges in spring to hunt pootys* and I was no less fond of robing the poor birds nests or searching among the prickly furze on the heath poking a stick into the rabbit holes and carefully observing when I took it out if there was down at the end which was a sign of a nest with young then in went the arm up to the shoulder and then fear came upon us that a snake might be conseald in the hole and then our bloods ran cold within us and startld us off to other sports

There is nothing but poetry about the existance of childhood real simple soul moving poetry the laughter and joy of poetry and not its philosophy and there is nothing of poetry about manhood but the reflection and the remembrance of what has been nothing more Thus it is that our play prolonging moon on spring evenings shed a richer lustre than the midday sun that surrounds us now in manhood for its poetical sunshine hath left us it is the same identical sun and we have learned to know that—for in boyhood every new day brought a new sun we knew no better and we was happy in our ignorance there is nothing of that new and refreshing sunshine upon the picture now it shines from the heavens upon real matter of fact existances and weary occupations The spring of our life—our youth—is the midsummer of our happiness—our pleasures are then real and heart stirring—they are but associations afterwards—where we laughed in childhood at the reality of the enjoyment felt we only smile in manhood at the reccolections of those enjoyments . . . we only feel the joy we possessed we see the daisy and love it because it was our first favourite in childhood when we sat upon the doorstep and cropt its smiling blossoms by the threshold we hear the nightingale and are

18

delighted because it was such a favourite in youth when the romance of beauty our first love stood in all the simplicity of woman in the moonlighting valley by our sides to listen the song—when sunday evenings came like the visits of angels and still the haunts of its annual visit are in the self same spots the paradise of our young hearts first extacys—green thickets where the leaves hide him from all but joys

The Village Boy

FREE from the cottage corner see how wild
The village boys along the pasture hies
With every smell and sound and sight beguiled
That round the prospect meets his wondering eyes
Now stooping eager for the cowslip peeps
As though hed get them all—now tired of these
Accross the flaggy brook he eager leaps
For some new flower his happy rapture sees
Now tearing mid the bushes on his knees
On woodland banks for blue bell flowers he creeps
And now while looking up among the trees
He spies a nest and down he throws his flowers
And up he climbs with new fed extacies
The happiest object in the summer hours

From *The Parish*

YOUNG farmer Bigg of this same flimsey class
Wise among fools and with the wise an ass
A farming sprout with more then farmers pride
Struts like the squire and dresses dignified
They call him squire at which his weakness aimd
But squires still view him as a fool misnamed
Yet dress and tattle ladys hearts can charm
And hes the choice with madams of the farm

Now with that lady strutting now with this
Braced up in stays as slim as sickly miss
Shining at christmass rout and vulgar ball
The favourite spark and rival of them all
And oft hell venture to bemean his pride
Tho bribes and mysterys do their best to hide
Teazing weak maidens with his pert deciet
Whose lives are humble but whose looks are sweet
Whose beauty happens to outrival those
With whom the dandy as an equal goes
Thus maids are ruined oft and mothers made
As if bewitchd without a fathers aid
Tho nodds and winks and whispers urge a guess
Weakness is bribed and hides its hearts distress
To live dishonoured and to dye unwed
For clowns grow jealous when theyre once misled
Thus pointed fingers brand the passing spark
And whispers often guess his deeds are dark
But friends deny and urge that doubts mislead
And prove the youth above so mean a deed
The town agrees and leaves his ways at will
A proud consieted meddling fellow still

Churchwardens Constables and Overseers
Makes up the round of Commons and of Peers
With learning just enough to sign a name
And skill sufficient parish rates to frame
And cunning deep enough the poor to cheat
This learned body for debatings meet
Tho natures marks are deep that all may scan
A knaves delusions from an honest man
Oppression often mourns the vile abuse
And flyes to justice—deemd of little use
Truth that coud once its own redresses seek
Is now deemd nothing and forbid to speek
Drove like an exile king from past renown
Power took its place and keeps it with a frown
And why shoud power or pride betray its trust
Is it too old a fashion to be just

Or does self interest inclinations bend
Aye aye the farmer is his worships friend
As parish priest from him he meets his tythes
Punctual as harvest wakes the tinkling scythes
Tho often grudgd yet he their hopes to glad
Prays better harvests when the last was bad
And as he deals so honestly with him
It must be malice in the poor or whim
Who seek relief and lay on them the blame
And hopeless seek it and return the same
Tho many heads the parliment prepare
And each one claims some wisdom for its share
Like midnight with her vapours tis so small
They make but darkness visible with all
Their secretary is the Parish Clerk
Whom like a shepherds dog they keep to bark
And gather rates and when the next are due
To cry them oer at church time from his pew
He as their 'Jack of all trades' steady shines
Thro thick and thin to sanction their designs
Who apes the part of King and Magistrate
And acts grant seginior of this turkish state
Who votes new laws to those already made
And acts by force when one is disobeyd
Having no credit which he fears to loose
He does whatever dirty jobs they chuse
Tasking the pauper labours [   ] to stand
Or clapping on his goods the Parish Brand
Lest he shoud sell them for the want of bread
On parish bounty rather pind then fed
Or carrying the parish book from door to door
Claiming fresh taxes from the needy poor
And if ones hunger overcomes his hate
And buys a loaf with what shoud pay the rate
He instant sets his tyrant laws to work
In heart and deed the essence of a turk
Brings summons for an eighteen penny rate
And gains the praises of the parish state
Or seizes goods and from the burthend clown

Extorts for extra trouble half a Crown
Himself a beggar that may shortly take
A weekly pittance from the rates they make
But the old proverb suits the subject well
Mount such on horseback and theyll ride to hell

And weres that lovley maid in days gone bye
The farmers daughter unreserved tho shye
That milked her cows and old songs used to sing
As red and rosey as the lovely spring
Ah these have dwindled to a formal shade
As pale and bedrid as my ladys maid
Who cannot dare to venture in the street
Some times thro cold at other times for heat
And vulgar eyes to shun and vulgar winds
Shrouded in veils green as their window blinds
These taught at school their stations to despise
And view old customs with disdainful eyes
Deem all as rude their kindred did of yore
And scorn to toil or foul their fingers more
Prim as the pasteboard figures which they cut
At school and tastful on the chimney put
They sit before their glasses hour by hour
Or paint unnatural daubs of fruit or flower
Or boasting learning novels beautys quotes
Or aping fashions scream a tune by notes
Een poetry in these high polished days
Is oft profained by their dislike or praise
Theyve read the Speaker till without a look
Theyll sing whole pages and lay bye the book
Then sure their judgment must be good indeed
When ere they chuse to speak of what they read
To simper tastful some devoted line
As somthing bad or somthing very fine
Thus mincing fine airs misconcieved at school
That pride outherods and compleats the fool
Thus housed mid cocks and hens in idle state
Aping at fashions which their betters hate
Affecting high lifes airs to scorn the past

Trying to be somthing makes them nought at last
These are the shadows that supply the place
Of famous daughters of the vanished race
And what are these rude names will do them harm
O rather call them 'Ladys of the Farm'
Miss Peevish Scornful once the Village toast
Deemd fair by some and prettyish by most
Brought up a lady tho her fathers gain
Depended still on cattle and on grain
She followd shifting fashions and aspired
To the high notions baffled pride desired
And all the profits pigs and poultry made
Were gave to Miss for dressing and parade
To visit balls and plays fresh hopes to trace
And try her fortune with a simpering face
And now and then in Londons crowds was shown
To know the world and to the world be known
All leisure hours while miss at home sojournd
Past in preparing till new routs returnd
Or tittle tattling oer her shrewd remarks
Of Ladys dresses or attentive sparks
How Mr So and So at such a rout
Fixed his eyes on her all the night about
While the good lady seated by his side
Behind her hands her blushes forced to hide
Till conscious Miss in pity she would say
For the poor lady turnd her face away
And young Squire Dandy just returned from france
How he first chose her from the rest to dance
And at the play how such a gent resignd
His seat to her and placed himself behind
How this squire bowd polite at her approach
And Lords een nodded as she passd their coach
Thus miss in raptures woud such things recall
And Pa and Ma in raptures heard it all
But when an equal woud his praise declare
And told young madam that her face was fair
She might believe the fellows truth the while
And just in sport might condescend to smile

But frownd his further teazing suit to shun
And deemd it rudeness in a farmers son
Thus she went on and visited and drest
And deemd things earnest that was spoke in jest
And dreamd at night oer prides uncheckd desires
Of nodding gentlemen and smiling squires
To Gretna green her visions often fled
And rattling coaches lumberd in her head
Till hopes grown weary with too long delay
Caught the green sickness* and declined away
And beauty like a garment worse for wear
Fled her pale cheek and left it much too fair
Then she gave up sick visits balls and plays
Were whispers turnd to anything but praise
All were thrown bye like an old fashiond song
Where she had playd show woman much too long
And condecended to be kind and plain
And 'mong her equals hoped to find a swain
Past follys now were hatful to review
And they were hated by her equals too
Notice from equals vain she tryd to court
Or if they noticed twas but just in sport
At last grown husband mad away she ran
Not with Squire Dandy but the servant man

Just as pride and fashion was creeping out of the citys like a plague to infest the Village Ralph Wormstall one of the last of the oppulent Farmers of the Old School flourished in his popularity whose fame for fat oxen and old Ale got wind even beyond the out skirts of the county   he was a very rich plain and superstitious man whose enemys called him 'horse Shoe Ralph' from a failing he had in believing in witches and a practice which he indulged in of nailing old horse shoes about the thresholds of his house and stables to prevail as a spell against their nightly depredations   he firmly believed that they rode his sheep trays and cow cribs about the yard on Winter nights and terrified himself and his horses till he tryed the above to prevent them which has branded the old farmer for ever with the name of 'Horse shoe Ralph' he was a plain rich old farmer and a good fellow in spite of his nick name and it was once whispered about the village that he got the Vicar to conjure some evil spirits in his cellar in a barrel of Ale which he fancied haunted his stock when his sheep dyed of the rot one wet season and his swine of the murrain in acorn time his enemys vouched it for truth and his friends did not contradict it but smiled when they heard it and calld it an 'innoscent weakness' be as it woud the Vicar was as superstitious as himself and always quoted the witch of Endor as a knockdown to unbelievers in witchcraft for he swallowed every story with the most credulous faith and because a farmer once doubted his authority of the 'witch of Endor' as a proof of their existance he instantly set him down as an Atheist and declared that he shoud not be buried in the churchyard if he could help it the old farmer was very rich but he never purchased a hunting horse and made it his boast among Sportsmen of confessing that he never followed a Fox in his life except to drive him from the henroost and seldom got astride of a saddle save when he gave old Dobbin a holiday from the plough to carry his Dame to the Fair to sell her Stilton cheese and while the young coxcomb was praising himself as a 'good shot' he woud confess it as a boast of being no Sportsman and considered it as a mark of his wisdom for such ignorance when they talked of their certificates to kill game he would cock his pipe higher and dryly observe that his Lordships Gamekeeper always sent a Hare at Christmass to his old tennants and he shoud be a fool to buy a certi-ficate to kill one—one Hare a year satisfied his wants and he fancied one liscence enabled them to shoot no more he was famous in Obstinacys and as famous for keeping them he kept an old Gun for no other purpose as it would seem then to hang among the fire Irons above the kitchen chimney but he found it useful to shoot sparrows in harvest and fright the Fox from the hen roost in Winter he always made it a rule to go to Market a foot and sold his Eggs and Butter himself as he thought it a better scheme then trusting to servants and he even took a pride to crack of his Orchard in good fruit years and sold both the Apples and Pears as he considered it a shame to devour any thing in his own house that might be done without and that woud turn into money he always sat at the same table at Harvest suppers with his men and would never suffer the Oven stove to be opend till the Vicar made his appearance When they shook hands drank a horn together as a pledge of thanks for a good harvest and then the supper was instantly on the table   he always made it a rule to sing all the songs he knew on that night which were not many and 'When this Old Hat was New' 'Toby Fillpot' and 'Speed the Plough' were always sung at a heat in quick succession for he never waited to be asked to sing or stopt to let any one else till he was done   and he prided himself in knowing 3 such good Songs for he coud not aspire to much praise in singing them as he had but a bad voice and readily acknowledged that his old friend the Vicar had a better who was fond of a song tho he always excused himself in a mixed company   and the old Farmer woud get him off by saying that he did it for the sake of his 'cloth' tho at the same time he woud urge him to say 'Chevey Chase' instead of singing it as there coud be no harm in that which he always readily agreed to   and he woud listen to any Song except the Vicar of Bray when he woud instantly get up though his pipe was just lighted and make excuse to leave the room which never happened at the old Farmers house where none offered to offend him for the old farmer woud not laugh at the Vicars expence tho he was fond of jokes and had two or three 'old Joe Millars'* which served for all seasons at which none laughd so heartily as himself   he always had his brown earthern pitcher of his old ale over a pipe after dinner and he never emptied it without drinking 'Long life to the King' tho 'peace and plenty' was his favourite toast in company and he felt it nessesary to appologize for its frequent use at his sunday dinner partys (for he never invited friends at another time except the vicar as he had no time to attend to them) by saying 'heres my old health gentlemen "Peace and Plenty" for want of a better' tho he thought at the same time that a better never existed and Vicar woud often confess so when he said it needed no appology

he was a great stickler for 'good old ways' as he called them and woud not suffer any of his family to reach a glass from the cupboard to drink out of when there was no company   and the old Vicar always joined him in believing that the clear horn with its silver rim was far better then glasses   and he seldom was in a passion with the wenches unless they wanted to follow the fashions and never thought his old dame a fool but once when she joind her daughters in thinking that a 'beautiful set of blue China' woud be a better ornament to the cupboard then the old Delf Teapot and white cups and saucers when he declared that they shoud all go without tea the instant they bought them whenever genteel company made glasses a nessesary appendage to the dinner table he appologized for the use of the old horn to himself by saying it was a gift of his mothers and he coud not discard it but his wife woud often let out his secret pregudice to glasses by laughing and saying that he never made it a rule to drink healths out of glasses and the old man woud laugh likewise as it gave him an opperturnity of begining up a long praise of his young days when horns and brown earthern ware pitchers were in fashion and if he was a little warm with liquor he would lay down his pipe without bidding and sing his old favourite 'When this old hat was new' the Daughters were often terribly anoyed with his meddlings in their dresses and his staunch canvasings for the old fashion of stays and stomachers and hair hanging down the back instead of being stuck up in combs but the Vicar sided for the girls dresses and thought it 'better for them to dress like other people then to go otherways' and the old dame woud finish the vicars story not giving time to say further—'and to be every bodys laughing stock' so they wearied his objections and he suffered them at last to go without stays and dress up their hair as they pleased tho he never woud agree to their follow-ing the 'Hoggs fashion' as he called it to wear ear rings so they were always obliged to wear caps in his presence to hide them when they talked of new fashions he woud instantly tell the history of his sunday suit which was a grey colored coat with hugh* buttons and a waistcoat of a same color with large pockets and flaps that hung over his hips big enough for a modern squires shooting jacket it was his 'wedding suit' and he seldom had it on without mentioning the surcumstance and his wife often declared to her guests tho her husband had been married 40 years that his sunday suit were as clean and as good as when they were first put on for the wedding this always made the old man smile and at the same time reach his hand to the shelf for the cloathsbrush to give it a stoke down his first wish had been to learn them all to be good Dairey wives by sending them to milk and do the kitchen work and make the cheese and butter themselves but his wife told the Vicar it was nothing but a mizardly* turn to save the wages of servants and ruin his daughters by making them fit for nothing but servants them selves the old Vicar woud laugh and say that her 'spark of pride' might be right enough for what he knew and she over ruled her husband against sending them to school by reminding him that Moll Huggings won a nobleman by the accomplishments she learned there so he let them go with the hopes of making them ladys   he was very cautious in remembering old customs and considerd the forgetting one an ill omen   he was always punctual in having the old bowl of frumitory* at sheep-shearing ready in time for the shepherds suppers and never let the old year go out without warming the old can of ale for the ringers well pepperd with ginger and he woud always have his Yule cake cut at Twelfth night for the Morris dancers to taste of with their beer let the old dame mutter as she might   he always got the fattest goose for Christmass and a couple of the best ducks in the yard for lammass tide and he kept almost every Saint day in the almanack with an additional pitcher after dinner and another pipe at night with the Vicar which he called 'honoring the day' and often remarked as they were all of the same 'cloth' with his good old neighbour (meaning the Vicar for he thought all the saints had been Vicars) they were worth remembering   and as the good old Vicar liked to wet his pipe in a moderate way he never once contradicted the custom or objected to catholics tho King Charles the Martyr and a few others by way of distinction were honoured with a prayer 'for the occasion' and a 'proper lesson' in the Bible read aloud to the family by the Vicar whom the old farmer always complimented as being the best reader in England   tho he did not pretend to much learning himself yet he fancied he coud read a chapter in the Bible with any man except the Vicar and he always made a point of reading one every sunday night aloud to his family and it was generaly from 'Proverbs' for he considered them as the finest parts of Scripture as he said a man coud not be made too wise for the world   the Vicar often tryed in vain to convince him that they aluded to spiritual conserns—for he never coud be beat out of his own way—as he said nothing had two mean-ings in his mind—so it was no use talking   he professed a little knowledge of books tho his whole acquai[n]tance took up no more then a spare corner on the mantlepiece were the Bible and Mores Almanack stood together which he considered two of the best books that were ever printed   there was the 'Whole duty of man' too which he prized as being a heir long* to the family and had belonged to his grandfather but he had never read it and Elliots Husbandry he had but he woud not confess that it was of any use to him and only kept as a family legacy for he used to say that farmers had done going school now adays and coud farm without Books at least ought to do with these lay a heap of pamphlets among which was the 'History of Jane Shore' 'The King and the Cobler' 'Johnny Armstrong' and a fragment of an old book on Cookery with 'Hamlet a tradegy by Will Shakspear Esqr' but these belongd to the Wife and the last to his daughters who woud often attempt to read passages of Shakspear on a winters evening to him a taste which they had brought from school— but they coud not beat him out of his old favourite opinion that 'George Barnwell' which his mother took him to see acted when a boy was a better play than 'Shakspear' for he always confounded the name with the subject and thought that Shakspear was the title of a Play the same as 'George Barnwell' and trying to correct his errors was of no use for he always stuck to his first opinions of things wether right or wrong he prided himself in such obst[i]nacys by calling those turncoats that were willing to be corrected out of their old opinions for so he called his errors they woud often try to get the Vicar on their side but he only confessed a dislike for Plays and stopt there tho the old Farmer had no knowledge of Poetry—'His music long had been the plough'—yet like a true Critic he was ever ready with his opinion in every thing and argued with the Vicars Latin as stoutly as if he had been at colledge half his life he was acquanted with Old Tussers Husbandry and set him down as the greatest poet on Earth and the Vicar shook his head in vain quoting scraps from Horace to prove him before Tusser tho nobody understood a word of the Latin but himself and the old farmer always fancied that if a man coud read english they coud read any thing if it was readable therefor he always called Horace a fool and his Latin nonsense because he coud not read it his Book of Old Tusser had been 'time out of mind' in his family and the favourite passages of his father were doubld down still as he left them at the 'lessons on Thrift' for his father had often called him 'the greatest poet that ever lived' and he deemed the book of sufficient importance to insert in his 'Will' as a family legacy which he 'desired might never go out of the family' nor was it placed on the corner shelf with the rest but carefully kept in his coffer with a piece of green bays stretched round the covers to preserve them the Vicar like his old neighbour was not much given to books he neither read much or pretended to it by talking about it his chief discourse was like the old farmers about markets and the weather and tho religion seldom shared their conversation the old farmer and his family were regular churchgoers

True to the Church no sunday shower
Kept him at home in that important hour

and he somtimes remarked to the Vicar over their pipes of his
never missing going to church of a Sunday but once in twenty years
and that was when he got his hay out of that meadow before the
'great July flood' came down for it was a memorable day with him
and he often wondered why Moor did not put it among the remarkable
things in his Almanack as well as the 'hot Wednesday' and tho those
who lost their hay blamed him for breaking the sabbath the Old
Vicar excused it and said he was right and preached a sermon in the
right of using urgent nessesitys the Vicar always stiled his neighbour
a rare churchman and wished the rest of his flock had attended as
regular and heeded as well to his counsels tho the old farmer thought
it no sin to talk about taxes in the porch or set the Clerk to give
notice to the congregation of new rates under the pulpit as soon as the
sermon was ended and this the Vicar agreed to as right likewise and
he was beloved in the Parish by most as he always prayed for fair or
wet weather as the farmer required . . . the Vicar was somtimes
disposed to be merry and would ramp* with the servant wenches in
hay time about the Cocks and rarely missed kissing them beneath the
missletoe at Christmass which he considered as a nessesary preface to
good luck thro the year for like his old neighbour he was a stickler for
old customs and it was whispered about the Village in his young
days that he was fond of women but when ever it was hinted to the
farmer's wife she woud fall in a passion and declare that he was as
honest a man as her husband

ᴐᴎᴐᴎᴐᴎ

The Cottager

TRUE as the church clock hand the hour pursues
He plods about his toils and reads the news
And at the blacksmiths shop his hour will stand
To talk of 'Lunun' as a foreign land
For from his cottage door in peace or strife
He neer went fifty miles in all his life

30

His knowledge with old notions still combined
Is fifty years behind the march of mind
He views new knowledge with suspicious eyes
And thinks it blasphemy to be so wise
Oer steams almighty tales he wondering looks
As witchcraft gleaned from old black leather books
Life gave him comfort but denied him wealth
He toils in quiet and enjoys his health
He smokes a pipe at night and drinks his beer
And runs no scores on tavern screens to clear
He goes to market all the year about
And keeps one hour and never stays it out
Een at St Thomas tide old Rovers bark
Hails Dapples trot an hour before its dark
He is a simple worded plain old man
Whose good intents take errors in their plan
Oft sentimental and with saddend vein
He looks on trifles and bemoans their pain
And thinks the angler mad and loudly storms
With emphasis of speech oer murdered worms
And hunters cruel—pleading with sad care
Pitys petition for the fox and hare
Yet feels self satisfaction in his woes
For wars crushed myriads of his slaughtered foes
He is right scrupelous in one pretext
And wholesale errors swallows in the next
He deems it sin to sing yet not to say
A song a mighty difference in his way
And many a moving tale in antique ryhmes
He has for christmass and such merry times
When chevy chase his master piece of song
Is said so earnest none can think it long
Twas the old Vicars way who should be right
For the late Vicar was his hearts delight
And while at church he often shakes his head
To think what sermons the old Vicar made
Downright and orthodox that all the land
Who had their ears to hear might understand
But now such mighty learning meets his ears

He thinks it greek or latin which he hears
Yet church recieves him every sabbath day
And rain or snow he never keeps away
All words of reverence still his heart reveres
Low bows his head when Jesus meets his ears
And still he thinks it blasphemy as well
Such names without a capital to spell
In an old corner cupboard by the wall
His books are laid—tho good in number small
His Bible first in place—from worth and age
Whose grandsires name adorns the title page
And blank leaves once now filled with kindred claims
Display a worlds epitome of names
Parents and childern and grandchildern—all
Memorys affections in the list recall
And Prayer book next much worn though strongly bound
Proves him a churchman orthodox and sound
The 'Pilgrims Progress' too and 'Death of Abel'
Are seldom missing from his sunday table
And prime old Tusser in his homely trim,
The first of Bards in all the world with him
And only poet which his leisure knows
—Verse deals in fancy so he sticks to prose
These are the books he reads and reads again
And weekly hunts the almanacks for rain
Here and no further learnings channels ran
Still neighbours prize him as the learned man
His cottage is a humble place of rest
With one spare room to welcome every guest
And that tall poplar pointing to the sky
His own hand planted when an idle boy
It shades his chimney while the singing wind
Hums songs of shelter to his happy mind
Within his cot the 'largest ears of corn'
He ever found his picture frames adorn
Brave Granbys Head—De Grasses grand defeat
He rubs his hands and tells how Rodney beat
And from the rafters upon strings depend
Bean stalks beset with pods from end to end

Whose numbers without counting may be seen
Wrote on the Almanack behind the screen
Around the corner upon worsted string
Pootys in wreaths above the cupboards hing
Memory at trifling incidents awakes
And there he keeps them for his childerns sakes
Who when as boys searched every sedgy lane
Traced every wood and shattered cloaths again
Roaming about on raptures easy wing
To hunt those very Pooty shells in spring
And thus he lives too happy to be poor
While strife neer pauses at so mean a door
Low in the sheltered valley stands his cot
He hears the mountain storm and feels it not
Winter and spring toil ceasing ere tis dark
Rests with the lamb and rises with the lark
Content is helpmate to the days employ
And care neer comes to steal a single joy
Time scarcely noticed turns his hair to grey
Yet leaves him happy as a child at play

Love and Memory

THOU art gone the dark journey
    That leaves no returning
Tis fruitless to mourn thee
    But who can help mourning
To think of the life
    That did laugh on thy brow
In the beautiful past
    Left so desolate now

When youth seemed immortal
    So sweet did it weave
Heavens haloo around thee
    Earths hopes to decieve

Thou fairest and dearest
   Where many were fair
To my heart thou art nearest
   Tho thy name is but there

The nearer the fountain
   More pure the stream flows
And sweeter to fancy
   The bud of the rose
And now thourt in heaven
   More pure is the birth
Of thoughts that wake of thee
   Then aught upon earth

As a bud green in spring
   As a rose blown in June
Thy beauty looked out
   And departed as soon
Heaven saw thee too fair
   For earths tennants of clay
And ere age did thee wrong
   Thou wert summoned away

I know thou art happy
   Why in grief need I be
Yet I am and the more so
   To feel its for thee
For thy presence possest
   As thy absence destroyed
The most that I loved
   And the all I enjoyed

So I try to seek pleasure
   But vainly I try
Now joys cup is drained
   And hopes fountain is dry
I mix with the living
   And what do I see
Only more cause for sorrow
   In loosing of thee

The year has its winter
  As well as its may
So the sweetest must leave us
  And the fairest decay
Suns leave us to night
  And their light none may borrow
So joy retreats from us
  Oertaken by sorrow

The sun greets the spring
  And the blossom the bee
The grass the blea* hill
  And the leaf the bare tree
But suns nor yet seasons
  As sweet as they be
Shall ever more greet me
  With tidings of thee

The voice of the cuckoo
  Is merry at noon
And the song of the nightingale
  Gladdens the moon
But the gayest to day
  May be saddest tomorrow
And the loudest in joy
  Sink the deepest in sorrow

But the lovely in death
  And the fairest must die
Fall once and for ever
  Like stars from the sky
So in vain do I mourn thee
  I know its in vain
Who could wish thee from joy
  To earths troubles again

Yet thy love shed upon me
  Life more then my own
And now thou art from me
  My being is gone

Words know not my grief
 Thus without thee to dwell
Yet in one I felt all
 When life bade thee farewell

Valentine—To Mary

THIS visionary theme is thine
From one who loves thee still
Tis writ to thee a valentine
But call it what you will
No more as wont thy beaming eye
To violets I compare
Nor talk about the lilys dye
To tell thee thou art fair

The time is past when hopes sweet will
First linked thy heart with mine
And the fond muse with simple skill
Chose thee its valentine
Though some may yet their powers employ
To wreath with flowers thy brow
With me thy loves a withered joy
With hope thourt nothing now

The all that youths fond spring esteems
Its blossoms plucked in may
Are gone like flowers in summer dreams
And thoughts of yesterday
The heavenly dreams of early love
Youths spell has broken there
And left the aching heart to prove
That earth owns nought so fair

Spring flowers were fitting hopes young songs
To grace loves earliest vow
But withered ones that autumn wrongs
Are emblems sweetest now

Their perished blooms that once were green
Hopes faded tale can tell
Of shadows were a sun hath been
And suit its memory well

Then why should I on such a day
Address a song to thee
When withered hope hath died away
And love no more can be
When blinded fate that still destroys
Hath rendered all as vain
And parted from the bosom joys
Twill never meet again

The substance of our joys hath been
Their flowers have faded long
But memory keeps the shadow green
And wakes this idle song
Then let esteem a welcome prove
That cant its place resign
And friendship takes the place of love
To send a valentine

[*Ballad: The spring returns the pewet screams*]

THE spring returns the pewet screams
Loud welcomes to the dawning
Though harsh and ill as now it seems
Twas music last may morning
The grass so green—the daisy gay
Wakes no joy in my bosom
Although the garland last may day
Wore not a finer blossom

For by this bridge my mary sat
And praised the screaming plover
As first to hail the day—when I
Confessed my self her lover

And at that moment stooping down
I pluckt a daisy blossom
Which smilingly she called her own
May garland for her bosom

And in her breast she hid it there
As true loves happy omen
Gold had not claimed a safer care
I thought loves name was woman
I claimed a kiss she laughed away
I sweetly sold the blossom
I thought myself a king that day
My throne was beautys bosom

And little thought an evil hour
Was bringing clouds around me
And least of all that little flower
Would turn a thorn to wound me
She showed me after many days
Though withered how she prized it
And then she leaned to wealthy praise
And my poor love despised it

Aloud the whirring pewet screams
The daisy blooms as gaily—
But where is Mary—absence seems
To ask that question daily—
No where on earth where joy can be
To glad me with her pleasure—
Another name she owns—to me
She is as stolen treasure

When lovers part—the longest mile
Leaves hope of some returning—
Though mines close bye—no hope the while
Within my heart is burning
One hour would bring me to her door
Yet sad and lonely hearted
If seas between us both should roar
We were not further parted

Though I could reach her with my hand
Ere suns the earth goes under
Her heart from mine—the sea and land
Are not more far asunder
The wind and clouds now here now there
Hold not such strange dominion
As womans cold perverted will
And soon estranged opinion

[*Love hearken the skylarks*]

LOVE hearken the skylarks
Right up in the sky
The suns on the hedges
The bushes are dry
Thy slippers unsullied
May wander abroad
Grass up to the ancles
Is dry as the road

There's the path if you chuse it
That wanders between
The wheat in the ear
And the blossoming bean
Where the wheat tyed accross
By some mischevous clown
Made you laugh though you tumbled
And stained your new gown

There's the larks brunny* eggs
In an old horses foot
In a nest made of twitches
And grasses and roots
We passed it last sunday
As I did to day
But thy foot skipt so lightly
It flew not away

39

And I feel thy discourse
And the beautiful tone
Of thy voice that made lonliness
More then alone
And it turned my heart inward
With joy like a pain
To think of our walk
As I went it again

The pewets are singing
An out o way song
But when beauty listens
The thrush wont be long
And as to the beautys
Thou'lt meet on the way
The hedges are loaded
With nothing but may

The swallows too twittring
And flittering away
Are just as if swimming
About in the hay
Where the wind dances over
And rolls up and down
And longs to be fanning
Thy holliday gown

The cuckoos* by handfuls
Peep up in the hay
And as to the crickets
They tinkle all day
And then theres the distance
Its steeples and trees
Fancy guesses them something
And neer dissagrees

For they give us a pleasure
And sweeten the talk
When a mere stone or hillock
Throws rest in the walk

And that old squatty oak
Where we rested and where
I first ventured secrets
Of love in thy ear

And more would have told thee
That Ive kept the whole week
For my courage turned chill
And my tongue could not speak
But I left thee so smiling
My fears are out grown
And hope waits to ask thee
When thou'lt be my own

[*Ive ran the furlongs to thy door*]

IVE ran the furlongs to thy door
And thought the way as miles
With doubts that I should see thee not
And scarcely staid for stiles
Lest thou should think me past the time
And change thy mind to go
Some other where to pass the time
The quickest speed was slow

But when thy cottage came in sight
And showed thee at the gate
The very scene was one delight
And though we parted late
Joy scarcely seemed a minute long
When hours their flight had taen
And parting welcomed from thy tongue
Be sure and come again

For thou wert young and beautiful
A flower but seldom found
That many hands were fain to pull
Who wouldnt care to wound

But there was no delight to meet
Where crowds and folly be
The fields found thee companion meet
And kept loves heart for me

To follys ear twas little known
A secret in a crowd
And only in the fields alone
I spoke thy name aloud
And if to cheer my walk along
A pleasant book was mine
Then beautys name in every song
Seemed nobodys but thine

Far far from all the world I found
Thy pleasant home and thee
Heaths woods a stretc[h]ing circle round
Hid thee from all but me
And o so green those ways when I
On sundays used to seek
Thy company they gave me joy
That cheered me all the week

And when we parted with the pledge
Right quickly to return
How lone the wind sighed through the hedge
Birds singing seemed to mourn
My old home was a stranger place
If told the story plain
My home was in thy happy face
That saw me soon again

[*Ballad: The sun had grown on lessening day*]

THE sun had grown on lessening day
A table large and round
And in the distant vapours grey
Seemed leaning on the ground

When Mary like a lingering flower
Did tenderly agree
To stay beyond her milking hour
And talk awhile with me

We wandered till the distant town
Had silenced nearly dumb
And lessend on the quiet ear
Small as a beetles hum
She turned her buckets upside down
And made us each a seat
And there we talked the evening brown
Beneath the rustling wheat

And while she milked her breathing cows
I sat beside the streams
In musing oer our evening joys
Like one in pleasant dreams
The bats and owls to meet the night
From hollow trees had gone
And een the flowers had shut for sleep
And still she lingered on

We mused in rapture side by side
Our wishes seemed as one
We talked of times retreating tide
And sighed to find it gone
And we had sighed more deeply still
Oer all our pleasures past
If we had known what now we know
That we had met the last

First Loves Recollections

FIRST love will with the heart remain
When all its hopes are bye
As frail rose blossoms still retain
Their fragrance till they die

And joys first dreams will haunt the mind
With shadows whence they sprung
As summer leaves the stems behind
On which springs blossoms hung

Mary I dare not call thee dear
Ive lost that right so long
Yet once again I vex thine ear
With memorys idle song
Had time and change neer blotted out
The love of former days
Thou wert the last that I should doubt
Of pleasing with my praise

When honied tokens from each tongue
Told with what truth we loved
How rapturous to thy lips I clung
Whilst nought but smiles reproved
But now methinks if one kind word
Were whispered in thine ear
Thoudst startle* like an untamed bird
And blush with wilder fear

How loath to part how fond to meet
Had we two used to be
At sunset with what eager feet
I hastened on to thee
Scarce nine days passed us ere we met
In spring nay winter weather
Now nine years suns have risen and set
Nor found us once together

Thy face was so familiar grown
Thy self so often nigh
A moments memory when alone
Would bring thee to mine eye
But now my very dreams forget
That witching look to trace
Though there thy beauty lingers yet
It wears a strangers face

I felt a pride to name thy name
But now that pride hath flown
My words een seem to blush for shame
That own I love thee on
I felt I then thy heart did share
Nor urged a binding vow
But much I doubt if thou couldst spare
One word of kindness now

Oh what is now my name to thee
Though once nought seemed so dear
Perhaps a jest in hours of glee
To please some idle ear
And yet like counterfeits with me
Impressions linger on
Tho all the gilded finery
That passed for truth is gone

Ere the world smiled upon my lays
A sweeter meed was mine
Thy blushing look of ready praise
Was raised at every line
But now methinks thy fervent love
Is changed to scorn severe
And songs that other hearts approve
Seem discord to thine ear

When last thy gentle cheek I prest
And heard thee feign adieu
I little thought that seeming jest
Would prove a word so true
A fate like this hath oft befell
Even loftier hopes then ours
Spring bids full many buds to swell
That neer can grow to flowers

The Cellar Door—A Ballad

By the old tavern door on the causway there lay
A hogshead of stingo* just rolled from a dray
And there stood the blacksmith awaiting a drop
As dry as the cinders that lay in his shop
And there stood the cobler as dry as a bun
Almost crackt like a bucket when left in the sun
He's wetted his knife upon pendil* and hone
Till hed not got a spittle to moisten the stone
So ere he could work though he'd lost the whole day
He must wait the new broach and bemoisten his clay

The cellar was empty each barrel was drained
To its dregs—and sir John like a rebel remained
In the street—for removal too powerful and large
For two or three topers to take into charge
Odd zooks said a tinker with bellows to mend
Had I strength I would just be for helping a friend
To walk on his legs but a child in the street
Had as much power as he to put John on his feet
Then up came the Blacksmith Sir Barley said he
I should just like to storm your old tower for a spree

And my strength for your strength and bar your renown
Id soon try your spirit by cracking your crown
And the cobler he tuckt up his apron and spit
In his hands for a burster but devil a bit
Would he move—so as yet they made nothing of land
For there lay the knight like a whale in the sand
Says the tinker if I could but drink of his veins
I should just be as strong and as stubborn again
Push along said the Toper the cellars adry
Theres nothing to moisten the mouth of a fly

Says the Host we shall burn out with thirst hes so big
Theres a cag* of small swipes* half as sour as a wig
In such like extreems why extreems will come pat
So lets een go and wet all our whistles with that

46

Says the tinker may I never bottom a chair
If I drink of small swipes while Sir Johns lying there
And the blacksmith he threw off his apron and swore
Small swipes should bemoisten his gullet no more
Let it out on the floor for the dry cock-a-roach
And he held up his hammer with threatens to broach

Sir John in his castle without leave or law
And suck out his blood with a reed or a straw
Ere hed soak at the swipes—and he turned him to start
Till the host for high treason came down a full quart
Just then passed the dandy and turned up his nose
They'd fain had him shoved but he looked at his cloaths—
And nipt his nose closer and twirled his stick round
And simpered tis nuisance to lie on the gound
But bacchus he laughed from the old tavern sign
Saying go on thou shadow and let the sun shine

Then again they all tried and the tinker he swore
That the hogshead had grown twice as heavy or more
Nay nay said the toper and reeled as he spoke
Were all getting weak thats the end of the joke
The ploughman came up and cut short his old tune
Hallooed 'woi' to his horses and though it was june
Said hed help them an hour ere hed keep them adry
'Well done' said the blacksmith with hopes running high
'He moves and by jingos success to the plough'
Aye aye said the cobler well conquer him now

The hogshead rolled forward the toper fell back
And the host laughed aloud as his sides they would crack
To see the old tinkers toil make such a gap
In his coat as to rend it from collar to flap
But the tinker he grunted and cried 'fiddle dee'
This garment hath been an old tennant with me
And a needle and thread with a little good skill
When Ive leisure will make it stand more weathers still
Then crack went his trunks from the hip to the knee
With his thrusting—no matter for nothing cared he

So long as Sir John rolled along to the door
Hes a chip of our block said the blacksmith and swore
And as sure as I live to drive nails in a shoe
He shall have at my cost a full pitcher or two
And the toper he hiccuped which hindered an oath
So long as he'd credit he'd pitcher them both
But the host stopt to hint when hed ordered the dray
Sir Barleycorns order was purchase and pay
And now the old knight is imprisoned and taen
To waste in the tavern mans cellar again

And now said the blacksmith let forfeits come first
For the insult swipes offered or his hoops I will burst
Here it is my old heartys—then drink your thirst full
Said the host for the stingo is worth a strong pull
Never fear for your legs if theyre broken to day
Winds only blow straws dust and feathers away
But the cask that is full like a jiant he lies
And jiants alone can his spirits capsize
If he lies in the path though a kings coming bye
John Barleycorns mighty and there he will lye

Then the toper sat down with a hiccup and felt
If he'd still an odd coin in his pocket to melt
And he made a wry face for his pocket was bare
—But he laughed and danced up 'what old boy are you
    there'
When he felt that a stiver* had got to his knee
Through a hole in his fob and right happy was he
Says the tinker Ive brawled till no breath I have got
And not met with twopence to purchase a pot
Says the toper Ive powder to charge a long gun
And a stiver Ive found when I thought I'd got none

So by helping a thirsty old friend in his need
Is my duty—take heart thou art welcome indeed
Then the smith with his tools in Sir John made a breach
And the toper he hiccuped and ended his speech

And pulled at the quart* till the snob he declared
When he went to drink next that the bottom was bared
No matter for that said the toper and grinned
I had but a soak and neer rested for wind
Thats low said the smith with a look rather vexed
But the quart was a forfiet so pay for the next

Then they talked of their skill and their labour till noon
When the sober mans toil was exactly half done
And there the plough lay—people hardly could pass
And the horses let loose pinsored up the short grass
And browsed on the bottle of flags* lying there
By the tinkers old budget* for mending a chair
The millers horse tyed to the old smithy door
Stood stamping his feet by the flies bitten sore
Awaiting the smith as he wanted a shoe
And he stampt till another fell off and made two

Till the miller expecting that all would get loose
Went to seek him and cursed him out right for a goose
But he dipt his dry beak in the mug once or twice
And forgot all his passion and toils in a trice
And the fly bitten horse at the old smithy post
Might stamp till his shoes and his legs they were lost
He sung his old songs and forgot his old mill
Blow winds high or low she might rest at her will
And the cobler in spite of his bustle for pelf
Left the shop all the day to take care of itself

And the toper who carried his house on his head
No wife to be teazing no bairns to be fed
Would sit out the week or the month or the year
Or a lifetime so long as he'd credit or beer
The ploughman he talked of his skill as divine
How he could plough furrows as straight as a line
And the blacksmith he swore had he but the command
He could shoe the kings hunter the best in the land
And the cobler declared was his skill but once seen
He should soon get an order for shoes from the queen

But the tinker he swore he could beat them all three
For gi me a pair of old bellows says he
And I'll make them roar out like the wind in a storm
And make them blow fire out of coals hardly warm
The toper said nothing but wished the quart full
And swore he could top it all off at a pull
Ha done said the tinker but wit was away
When the bet was to bind him he'd nothing to pay
And thus in the face of lifes sun and shower weather
They drank bragged and sung and got merry together

The sun it went down—the last gleam from his brow
Flung a smile of repose on the holiday plough
The glooms they approached and the dews like a rain
Fell thick and hung pearls on the old sorrel mane
Of the horse that the miller had brought to be shod
And the morning awoke saw a sight rather odd
For a bit of the halter still hung at the door
Bit through by the horse now at feed on the moor
And the old tinkers budget lay still in the weather
While all kept on singing and drinking together

February—A Thaw

THE snow is gone from cottage tops
The thatch moss glows in brighter green
And eves in quick succession drops
Where grinning icles once hath been
Pit patting wi a pleasant noise
In tubs set by the cottage door
And ducks and geese wi happy joys
Douse in the yard pond brimming oer

The sun peeps thro the window pane
Which children mark wi laughing eye
And in the wet street steal again
To tell each other spring is nigh

And as young hope the past recalls
In playing groups will often draw
Building beside the sunny walls
Their spring-play-huts of sticks or straw

And oft in pleasures dreams they hie
Round homsteads by the village side
Scratting the hedgrow mosses bye
Where painted pooty shells abide
Mistaking oft the ivy spray
For leaves that come wi budding spring
And wondering in their search for play
Why birds delay to build and sing

The milkmaid singing leaves her bed
As glad as happy thoughts can be
While magpies chatter oer her head
As jocund in the change as she
Her cows around the closes stray
Nor lingering wait the foddering boy
Tossing the molehills in their play
And staring round in frolic joy

Ploughmen go whistling to their toils
And yoke again the rested plough
And mingling oer the mellow soils
Boys' shouts and whips are noising now
The shepherd now is often seen
By warm banks oer his work to bend
Or oer a gate or stile to lean
Chattering to a passing friend

Odd hive bees fancying winter oer
And dreaming in their combs of spring
Creeps on the slab beside their door
And strokes its legs upon its wing
While wild ones half asleep are humming
Round snowdrop bells a feeble note
And pigions coo of summer coming
Picking their feathers on the cote

The barking dogs by lane and wood
Drive sheep afield from foddering ground
And eccho in her summer mood
Briskly mocks the cheery sound
The flocks as from a prison broke
Shake their wet fleeces in the sun
While following fast a misty smoke
Reeks from the moist grass as they run

Nor more behind his masters heels
The dog creeps oer his winter pace
But cocks his tail and oer the fields
Runs many a wild and random chase
Following in spite of chiding calls
The startld cat wi harmless glee
Scaring her up the weed green walls
Or mossy mottld apple tree

As crows from morning perches flye
He barks and follows them in vain
Een larks will catch his nimble eye
And off he starts and barks again
Wi breathless haste and blinded guess
Oft following where the hare hath gone
Forgetting in his joys excess
His frolic puppy days are done

The gossips saunter in the sun
As at the spring from door to door
Of matters in the village done
And secret newsings mutterd oer
Young girls when they each other meet
Will stand their tales of love to tell
While going on errands down the street
Or fetching water from the well

A calm of pleasure listens round
And almost whispers winter bye
While fancy dreams of summer sounds
And quiet rapture fills the eye

The sun beams on the hedges lye
The south wind murmurs summer soft
And maids hang out white cloaths to dry
Around the eldern skirted croft

Each barns green thatch reeks in the sun
Its mate the happy sparrow calls
And as nest building spring begun
Peeps in the holes about the walls
The wren a* sunny side the stack
Wi short tail ever on the strunt*
Cockd gadding up above his back
Again for dancing gnats will hunt

The gladdend swine bolt from the sty
And round the yard in freedom run
Or stretching in their slumbers lye
Beside the cottage in the sun
The young horse whinneys to its mate
And sickens from the threshers door
Rubbing the straw yards banded gate
Longing for freedom on the moor

Hens leave their roosts wi cackling calls
To see the barn door free from snow
And cocks flye up the mossy walls
To clap their spangld wings and crow
About the steeples sunny top
The jackdaw flocks resemble spring
And in the stone archd windows pop
Wi summer noise and wanton wing

The small birds think their wants are oer
To see the snow hills fret again
And from the barns chaff litterd door
Betake them to the greening plain
The woodmans robin startles coy
Nor longer at his elbow comes
To peck wi hungers eager joy
Mong mossy stulps* the litterd crumbs

Neath hedge and walls that screen the wind
The gnats for play will flock together
And een poor flyes odd hopes will find
To venture in the mocking weather
From out their hiding holes again
Wi feeble pace they often creep
Along the sun warmd window pane
Like dreaming things that walk in sleep

The mavis thrush wi wild delight
Upon the orchards dripping tree
Mutters to see the day so bright
Spring scraps of young hopes poesy
And oft dame stops her burring wheel
To hear the robins note once more
That tutles while he pecks his meal
From sweet briar hips beside the door

The hedghog from its hollow root
Sees the wood moss clear of snow
And hunts each hedge for fallen fruit
Crab hip and winter bitten sloe
And oft when checkd by sudden fears
As shepherd dog his haunt espies
He rolls up in a ball of spears
And all his barking rage defies

Thus nature of the spring will dream
While south winds thaw but soon again
Frost breaths upon the stiffening stream
And numbs it into ice—the plain
Soon wears its merry garb of white
And icicles that fret at noon
Will eke their icy tails at night
Beneath the chilly stars and moon

Nature soon sickens of her joys
And all is sad and dumb again
Save merry shouts of sliding boys
About the frozen furrowd plain

The foddering boy forgets his song
And silent goes wi folded arms
And croodling* shepherds bend along
Crouching to the whizzing storms

Valentine Eve

Young girls grow eager as the day retires
And smile and whisper round their cottage fires
Listning for noises in the dusky street
For tinkling latches and for passing feet
The prophecys of coming joys to hark
Of wandering lovers stealing thro' the dark
Dropping their valentines at beautys door
With hearts and darts and love knots littered oer
'Aye' said a gossip by a neighbours hearth
While the young girls popt up in tittering mirth
To hear the door creak with heart jumping signs
And footsteps hastening bye and valentines
Drop rustling on the floor—'aye aye' she said
As they kept back and smiled oer what they read
'Your fine love letters might be worth your smiles
If 'stead of coming from some creeping giles
Rich lovers sent them as it once befell
To one young maiden I remember well
Tho Madam Meers now lives at Oakley Hall
With coach and four and footmen at her call
Her father was none else than farmer Ling
And she plain Kate before she wore a ring
Tho I began about the valentine
The starting subject I'll awhile resign
But hear with patience and ye'll quickly learn
For I'll haste on and take it up in turn
   When the poor irish from their country rove
And like scotch cattle throng the road in droves
To seek the profits which the harvest brings
At that same season to old farmer Lings

A stranger came but not of foreign blood
He spoke plain english and his looks was good
And hired himself for toil the season thro
At any jobs the harvest had to do
And tho he seemed as merry as the clowns*
He neer was noisey like such vulgar lowns*
And when he heard them urge a vulgar joke
At passing maids he neither laughd nor spoke
But while he saw the blush their rudeness made
His manners seemed their freedom to upbraid
For hed turn round a moment from his toil
And say 'good morning' and would kindly smile
Tho dressed like them in jacket russet brown
His ways betrayed him better than a clown
And many a guess from rumours whispers fell
And gossips daily had new tales to tell
Some said he once had been a wealthy man
And from a bankrupts painful ruin ran
Others with far worse causes marked his flight
And taxed him with a forgers name out right
And tho he heard such whispers passing bye
Hed laugh but never stop to question why
Nor seemed offended think whatere he would
But always seemed to be in merry mood
Bad as folks thought him I was well aware
That he by one at least was welcome there
Who always mid their noisey idle prate
Would silent stand and that was rosey Kate
She seemed bewitched with his good mannered ways
And never spoke about him but to praise
She was the youngest daughter fair and gay
As flowers that open in the dews of May
Loves heart neer trembled at a sweeter face
When health and beauty courted its embrace
Nor lived a merrier girl beneath the sun
For romp and play when labours work was done
Wild as a Doe that overleapt the park
She'd laugh and play oer evenings games till dark
All noise and stir like an ill sitting hen

But shoy* and timid in the sight of men
Her friends neer dreamed of what all else might see
His ways was plain as the 'cross row'* to me
When ere he caught her in her dissabille
Washing or aught—she ran as lovers will
Up stairs as quickly as she could from sight
To seek her glass and put her garments right
Anxious to meet him in her best attire
As he the more might love her and admire
And once at eve as we the cows did wait
He leaned beside her on the stackyard gate
And smiled and whispered as she stooped adown
To pull some burdocks from her sweeping gown
'Mary theres one whose thoughts when your away
'Always cling with you full as close as they
'Who hopes yet fears his growing love to name
'Lest you should throw it from you just the same'
She coloured like the fire and turned aside
But I saw quickly what her heart would hide
And up and told her when she milked at night
That be the harvest stranger who he might
A winning tongue neath toils disguise was hid
That knew more manners then our farmers did
She laughd and said 'Aye so you love him then
But as for her shed no regard for men'
Tho such denials kept the secret worse
I took no heed but sanctioned her discourse
And when she dressed to walk on harvest eves
Spending an hour to glean among the sheaves
Things were to others eyes full often seen
That she'd more errands then the one to glean
She always followed in the strangers toil
Who oft would stop to wet his hook and smile
And loose when none percieved from out his hand
Some wheat ears now and then upon the land
And oft when running from a sudden shower
Or leaving off to take their beavering hour
He always from the rest would linger last
To leave a smile and greet her as he past

All that had any sense to use their eyes
Might easy guess beneath the thin disguise
Like to the burr* about the moon at night
It seems to covert* but still leaves it light
And sure enough he was a handsome swain
One any maiden had been proud to gain
Een I have often envied Kittys place
And felt the heartache at his smiling face
For when I passed him he would always smile
And often took my milk pail oer a stile
Jeering us both of sweethearts in our play
Tho nothing but in good behaviours way
He said to me—yet without shame I say't
I thought myself as fine a wench as Kate
Dark as the strangers mystery were his ways
He wandered round the field on sabbath days
And left to vulgar minds the noisey town
Nor made a partner of a fellow clown
Tracing the wood tracks over grown with moss
Or with heath rabbits winding thro the goss*
And oft neath blackthorn shadows by the brook
Was seen by shepherds musing oer a book
And in his button holes was always seen
Wild flowers—that in his rambles he would glean
Folks often marvelled at each seeming whim
What we thought weeds seemed best of flowers with him
The ragged robin by the runnel brinks
Seemed in his eye much finer flowers then pinks
And tall wild woad that lifts its spirey* tops
By stone pits—nay een briony and hops
He would from hedges in a poesy* bind
And leave the woodbine and the rose behind
All wondered at his ways and some believed
The man was crazed but rumour gets decieved
     When busy harvest to its end had come
And children ran to hollow* 'harvest home'
Bawling half hidden neath each green ash bough
For cross plumb skittles* out of fashion now
Kate was the queen upon that merry night

58

And rode upon the waggon drest in white
The stranger half looked up to see her stand
And smiling called her 'queen of fairey land'
That harvest supper we had morts* of fun
And Farmer Sparks was there a neighbours son
He was her fathers choice who dreamed of gain
And talked of marriage as he would of grain
He vainly tryed young Kittys smiles to share
And next her without bidding took his chair
Full oft with gracious simperings looking up
To drink to Kitty oer the silver cup
While she but with a careless look replied
Or turned like one that would not heed aside
But if the stranger gazed above his horn
She smiled as lovely as a may day morn
Soon as the racket and the fun began
Young Farmer Sparks up from the table ran
To act the crane* and poked the room about
Breaking the pipes and putting candles out
While wenches squealed and old dames fainted pale
Quickly recovering with an horn of ale
The stranger seemed to shun the rude uproar
And Kate slove* with him to the kitchen door
I sat on thorns the live long night about
For fear their ways would blab the secret out
And had aught met the fathers jealous sight
Farewell to fun and frolic for the night
But all went right and naught was seen or done
To spoil the acting or to damp the fun
The old man smoked his pipe and drank his ale
And laughed most hearty at each sport and tale
On the next day for Kate a gloomy day
The harvest labourers took their parting pay
And the young stranger with a downcast eye
Turned round to Kate and bade us both 'good bye'
Soon as he went she ran with eager feet
Up stairs to see him vanish down the street
I heard the creeking casement open thrown
And knew full well what she neer cared to own

For her swelled eyes their secrets badly kept
When she came down they told me she had wept
Twas harmless sorrows did her bosom move
And theres no sin nor shame to weep for love
Sometimes she seemd as sad and sometimes gay
But never more appeared so fond of play
Lone pastimes now did leisure hours engage
Dull as a tame bird wonted to the cage
She seemed to be while time unheeding went
Nor left a hope to ease her discontent
   At length the postman with his wind pluft* cheek
That brought the news and letters once a week
Some mornings after valentine was bye
Came in and gan his parcel to untie
Her sisters bustled up and smiling thought
That he some lovers valentines had brought
But hopes with them was quickly out of date
Soon as they found the letter was for Kate
Poor wench her colour came and went away
Now red as crimson then as pale as may
The old man thought it farmer Sparkes's son
That sent the thing and felt his wishes won
Laying his pipe down he began to joke
And clapt her on the shoulder as he spoke
'Have at him wench thats all I have to tell
'And bonny Kate will sell her beauty well
'For he's got money wench as well as love
'To make your ring sit easy as a glove'
But when he found the postmark and the seal
Did different notions to his own reveal
He let the mystery undisturbed remain
And turned his chair and took his pipe again
Her sisters bit their lips in silent spite
And could not keep their envy out of sight
To think that bonny Kate above them all
Who never in her life had seen a ball
Nor spent an hour to curl her parted hair
Nor of her beauty seemed to have one care
That romped about at play and joined in toil

While they would sit and not a finger soil
Should be thus noticed—but they urged a doubt
And muttered some low bred ingenious* lout
Had sent the thing and said with louder voice
'Be who he will he wears a vulgar choice'
And tho they might clowns valentines condemn
Een they were welcome when they came to them
For Sawney* Sparks and each young farmer guest
Was little better then a clown at best
Be who he might it made their bosoms ache
And worse when time unriddled their mistake

Kate had no pride about her she was free
As any maiden in the world could be
And while her sisters dressed in muslin gowns
And scorned on holidays to talk with clowns
She seemed to wear no better dress then I
Yet won a look from every passer bye
And some that passed would mutter praises loud
'Theres a sweet face' which never made her proud
She made all equals—used een beggars well
And all of Kate had some kind things to tell

When summer eves the first come swallows meet
As Kate and I were looking down the street
These little summer visitors to view
Marking how lowley and how swift they flew
We heard the bustle of a coach and four
Race the lane dust and hurry towards the door
The yard dog never barked nor made a fuss
But dropt his tail and stopt to gaze with us
Een the old geese were silent at the sight
And in amazement half forgot their spite
The noisey childern in the streets at play
Picked up their tops and taws* and sneaked away
And Kate half startled sneaked and hurried in
While wonder heaved her bosom to her chin
And well it might for twas the very same
Man that at harvest as a reaper came
The same that sent her at the valentine
The clever letter that was wrote so fine

Old women that had muttered round the town
And called the stranger by worse names then clown
Peeped out and dropped their courtseys* to the coach
And mixed in groups to question its approach
Fine as he was soon as he came in view
I knew his face and so did Kitty too
Who overcame turned white as was the wall
And almost fainted but he stopt the fall
And kept her in his arms with fondling pain
Till the fresh rose came to her face again
Her father gaped and wondered at the throng
And bowed and chattered wether right or wrong
Guessing that love was what the stranger meant
The coach was plenty to buy his consent
And thinking Kate had made her fortune now
He bustled up and gan to scrape and bow
And bade Kate welcome in her noble guest
With wine and ale the oldest and the best
But he was not to be by flattery fed
He only smiled and never turned his head
I want no formal welcomes keep your place
Old man he said—But why that blushing face
My bonny Kate I left thee fond and true
And wish to find thee as I used to do
Smiling and free as on each harvest morn
When I as labourer reaped thy fathers corn
I travelled in disguise alone to find
The native undisguise of womans mind
Theyre easy coyed* to take a golden bait
And love in mockery—but my bonny Kate
I found in thee a heart I wished to prove
Who ignorant of wealth was caught by love
Then shrink not if thy heart is still sincere
Nor blush nor startle with confounding fear
To see thy mother at this finery awed
And father bow and christen me 'my lord'
No honours and no titled names are mine
But all I have plain love and wealth is thine
Tho I have grown above thy fathers toil

In reaping corn and ploughing up the soil
Yet that fond love my Kitty showed to me
Was neer a moment from my memory
Thy beauty would bewitch a world with love
And I've returned thy worth and vows to prove
Ive came as promised for thee many a mile
Then bid me welcome with thy usual smile
Reach not sweet Kate the silver cup for me
But bring the horn toil often drank to thee
And thus he said but how can words of mine
Relate a speech that he told oer so fine
However there they sat the night about
And drank the old brown pitcher nearly out
Kate often smiled but yet was still and shoy
And the old man got down right drunk for joy
Who often reached across his elbow chair
To gain the whisper of his daughters ear
Muttering when ere the stranger turned his head
His urgent wishes in her looks to wed
Fingers in vain were shook to keep him still
He een got wilder in his head strong will
'—A good receipt neer makes a bargain wrong
'So Kate says he burn nothing with your tongue'
And drank her health anew—the strangers eye
Looked smiling at him but made no reply
When morning came Kate gave her hearts consent
The coach was ordered and to church they went
Before the sun the old man bustled up
And gave his blessing oer the silver cup
At the glad closing of that happy day
The stranger drove his blooming bride away
She left her presents for the cake and tea
Leaving old gossips in the highest glee
While he with gifts the ringers did regale
Who rung his praises both with bells and ale
And tho she promised me a handsome gown
When eer she married be he gent or clown
No wonder that her memory was away
I quite excused her breaking it that day

He was no lord tho he was full as great
A country squire with a vast estate
In the most trifling things she had her ends
And ere she'd gone a twelvemonth from her friends
She wished once more to see us all again
And as indulgence to her lonely pain
They in their coach and four came shining down
To rent a dwelling near her native town
And Oakley Hall that tops old Cromwells hill
He took to please and occupys it still
A fine old place with ivy round the porch
That long had stood as empty as a church
Folks say it had a Cromwells castle been
And in the walls still cannon holes are seen
There they in happiness and luxury live
And share the all lifes pleasure has to give
Sometimes they visit at their own estate
And yearly drive to London with the great
 Whenever I have errands from the town
To seek the hall she gives me many a crown
Making me welcome in plain friendly ways
And often laughs about our younger days
Hark thats the clock well I must up and roam
My man no doubt sits waiting me at home
Wholl scold and say by sitting here till nine
That Im an old fool keeping Valentine
So good night all' and hastening from her seat
She sought her clogs and clocked* adown the street
The girls were glad twas done—and in her place
The happy cat leapt up and cleaned her face
While crickets that had been unheard so long
Seemed as she stopt to start a merrier song

ererer

I DO NOT know how to class the venemous animals further then by
the vulgar notion of putting toads common snakes black snakes—
calld by the Peasantry Vipers—Newts (often calld eatherns) and a
nimble scaly looking newt-like thing about the heaths calld Swifts*

by the furze kidders* and cow keepers   all these we posses in troubl-
some quantitys all of which is reckond poisonous by the common
people tho a many daring people has provd that the common snake
is not for I have seen men with whom I have workd in the fields take
them up and snatch them out of joint as they calld it in a moment so
that when they was thrown down they coud not stir but lay and
dyd   others will take them up in one hand and hold the other agen
that double pointed fang which they put out in a threatning manner
when pursued and which is erroniously calld their sting and when it
touches the hand it appears utterly harmless and turns again as weak
as an horse hair   yet still they are calld poisonous and dreaded by
many people and I myself cannot divest my feelings of their first
impressions tho I have been convincd to the contrary we have them
about us in great quantitys   they even come in the village and breed
in the dunghills in farm yards and harbour in old walls   they are fond
of lying rolld up like a whipthong in the sun   they seem to be always
jealous of danger as they never lye far from their hiding places
and retreat in a moment at the least noise or sound of approaching
feet   they lay a great number of eggs white and large   the shell is a
skinny substance and full of a glutiness matter like the white in birds
eggs   they hang together by hundreds as if strung on a string   they lay
them on the south side of old dunghills were the heat of the sun and
the dung together hatches them   when they first leave the shells they
are no thicker then a worsted needle or bodkin   they nimble* about
after the old snakes and if they are in danger the old ones open their
mouths and the young dissapear down their throats in a moment till
the danger is over and then they come out and run about as usual   I
have not seen this myself but I am as certain of it as if I had because
I have heard it told so often by those that did when I have been
pilling* bark in the woods in oaking time   I have seen snakes creeping half errect by the sides of the fallen oaks that were pilld putting
their darting horse hair like tongue every now and then to the tree
and I was a long while ere I could make out what they were doing but
I made it out at last in my mind that they were catching flyes that
were attracted there in great quantitys to the moister of the sap just
after the bark had been ripd off   this I have observd many times and
I think if it were examind they have a sticky moister at the end of
those double ended fangs that appear like a bit of wailbone split at
the end or a double horse hair which attaches to the flye as soon as

touchd like bird lime and I think this is the use for which nature designd their mistaken stings   the motion was so quick that the prey which it seizd coud not be percievd when taken but I have not the least doubt that such was its object   people talk about the Water-snake but I cannot believe otherwise then that the water and land snake are one tho I have killd snakes by the water in meadows of a different and more deep color then those I have found in the fields the water snake will swallow very large frogs   I have often known them to be ripd out of their bellys by those who have skind the snake to wear the skin round their hats which is reckond as a charm against the headach and is often tryd but with what success I am not able to say . . . when the french prisoners were at Norman cross Barracks it was a very common thing among the people of the villages round to go in the fens a snake catching and carry home large sticks of them strung like eels on osiers which the French men woud readily buy as an article of very palatable food . . . the common snake is very fond of milk and it often makes its way into a dairy by a mouse hole or some other entrance to sip the cream—in the fens (were they are as numerous as flies) they will creep up the milk pails that are set to cool at the door of an evening by 3 or four together

PASTORAL poems are full of nothing but the old thread bare epithets of 'sweet singing cuckoo' 'love lorn nightingale' 'fond turtles' 'sparkling brooks' 'green meadows' 'leafy woods' etc etc   these make up the creation of Pastoral and descriptive poesy and every thing else is reckond low and vulgar   in fact they are too rustic for the fashion-able or prevailing system of ryhme till some bold inovating genius rises with a real love for nature and then they will no doubt be considerd as great beautys which they really are

THE encouragment my first Volume met with lifted me up into heartsome feelings and ryhming was continually with me night and day   I began the Village Minstrel a long while before attempting to describe my own feelings and love for rural objects and I then began in good earnest with it   after the trial of my first poems was made and compleated it was little time but I was still unsatisfied with it and am now and often feel sorry that I did not withold it a little longer for revision   the reason why I dislike it is that it does not describe the feelings of a ryhming peasant strongly or localy enough

I BELIEVE that the habits of the land rail or landrake and the Quail are little known   in fact I know but little of them myself but that little is at your pleasure   Were is the school boy that has not heard that mysterious noise which comes with the spring in the grass and green corn   I have followd it for hours and all to no purpose   it seemd like a spirit that mockd my folly in running after it   the noise it makes is a low craking very much like that of a Drake from whence I suppose it got the name of Landrake   I never started it up when a boy but I have often seen it flye since   about two years ago while I was walking in a neighbours homstead we heard one of these landrails in his wheat   we hunted down the land and accidentily as it were we started it up   it seemd to flye very awkard and its long legs hung down as if they were broken   it was just at dewfall in the evening   it flew towards the street instead of the field and popt into a chamber window that happend to be open when a cat seizd and killd it   it was somthing like the quail but smaller and very slender with no tail scarcly and rather long legs   it was of a brown color   they lay like the quail and partridge upon the ground in the corn and grass   they make no nest but scrat a hole in the ground and lay a great number of eggs   My mother found a landrails nest once while weeding wheat with seventeen eggs and they were not sat on   they were short eggs made in the form of the partridges not much unlike the color of the plovers   I imagine the young run with 'the shells on their heads' as they say by partridges and plovers for most of these ground hatchd birds do . . . the year before last I was helping to carry yaumd* beans which are shorn with a hook instead of being mown with a scythe and stoukd in shoves like wheat   as I was throwing one of these shoves* upon the waggon somthing ran from under it very quick and squat- ted about the land   I mistook it at first for a rat as it hastend bye me and struck at it with my fork but on percieving my mistake I stoopd down to catch it   it awkardly took wing and settld in a border of bush   I found it was a landrail by its legs dangling down as it flew

∽∽∽∽

67

The Wren

WHY is the cuckoos melody preferred
And nightingales sick song so madly praised
In poets ryhmes is there no other bird
In natures minstrelsy that hath not raised
Ones heart to extacy and mirth as well
I judge not how anothers taste is caught
With mine theres other birds that bear the bell
Whose song hath crowds of happy memorys brought
Such is the robin singing in the dell
And little wren that many a time hath sought
Shelter from showers in huts where I did dwell
At early spring the tenant of the plain
Keeping my sheep and still they come to tell
The happy storys of the past again

The Fern Owls Nest

THE weary woodman rocking* home beneath
His tightly banded faggot wonders oft
While crossing over the furze crowded heath
To hear the fern owls cry that whews* aloft
In circling whirls and often by his head
Wizzes as quick as thought and ill at rest
As through the rustling ling* with heavy tread
He goes nor heeds he tramples near its nest
That underneath the furze or squatting thorn
Lies hidden on the ground and teazing round
That lonely spot she wakes her jarring noise
To the unheeding waste till mottled morn
Fills the red east with daylights coming sounds
And the heaths echoes mocks the herding boys

Sand Martin

THOU hermit haunter of the lonely glen
And common wild and heath—the desolate face
Of rude waste landscapes far away from men
Where frequent quarrys give thee dwelling place
With strangest taste and labour undeterred
Drilling small holes along the quarrys side
More like the haunts of vermin than a bird
And seldom by the nesting boy descried
Ive seen thee far away from all thy tribe
Flirting* about the unfrequented sky
And felt a feeling that I cant describe
Of lone seclusion and a hermit joy
To see thee circle round nor go beyond
That lone heath and its melancholly pond

To the Snipe

LOVER of swamps
The quagmire over grown
With hassock tufts of sedge—where fear encamps
Around thy home alone

The trembling grass
Quakes from the human foot
Nor bears the weight of man to let him pass
Where thou alone and mute

Sittest at rest
In safety neath the clump
Of hugh flag forrest that thy haunts invest
Or some old sallow stump

Thriving on seams
That tiney island swell
Just hilling from the mud and rancid streams
Suiting thy nature well

For here thy bill
Suited by wisdom good
Of rude unseemly length doth delve and drill
The gelid* mass for food

And here mayhap
When summer suns hath drest
The moors rude desolate and spungy lap
May hide thy mystic nest

Mystic indeed
For isles that ocean make
Are scarcely more secure for birds to build
Then this flag hidden lake

Boys thread the woods
To their remotest shades
But in these marshy flats these stagnant floods
Security pervades

From year to year
Places untrodden lie
Where man nor boy nor stock hath ventured near
—Nought gazed on but the sky

And fowl that dread
The very breath of man
Hiding in spots that never knew his tread
A wild and timid clan

Wigeon and teal
And wild duck—restless lot
That from mans dreaded sight will ever steal
To the most dreary spot

Here tempests howl
Around each flaggy plot
Where they who dread mans sight the water fowl
Hide and are frighted not

Tis power divine
That heartens them to brave
The roughest tempest and at ease recline
On marshes or the wave

Yet instinct knows
Not safetys bounds—to shun
The firmer ground where sculking fowler goes
With searching dogs and gun

By tepid springs
Scarcely one stride accross
Though brambles from its edge a shelter flings
Thy safety is at loss

And never chuse
The little sinky foss
Streaking the moores whence spa-red waters spews
From pudges fringed with moss

Free booters there
Intent to kill and slay
Startle with cracking guns the trepid air
And dogs thy haunts betray

From dangers reach
Here thou art safe to roam
Far as these washy flag grown marshes stretch
A still and quiet home

In these thy haunts
Ive gleaned habitual love
From the vague world where pride and folly taunts
I muse and look above

Thy solitudes
The unbounded heaven esteems
And here my heart warms into higher moods
And dignifying dreams

I see the sky
Smile on the meanest spot
Giving to all that creep or walk or flye
A calm and cordial lot

Thine teaches me
Right feelings to employ
That in the dreariest places peace will be
A dweller and a joy

The March Nightingale

Now sallow* catkins once all downy white
Turn like the sunshine into golden light
The rocking clown leans oer the spinny rail
In admiration at the sunny sight
The while the blackcap doth his ears assail
With a rich and such an early song
He stops his own and thinks the nightingale
Hath of her monthly reckoning counted wrong
'Sweet jug jug jug' comes loud upon his ear
Those sounds that unto may by right belong
Yet on the awthorn scarce a leaf appears
How can it be—spell struck the wandering boy
Listens again—again the sound he hears
And mocks it in his song for very joy

THE Gloworm is a sort of catterpillar insect and thousands of them may be seen on Casterton Cowpasture on a summer night they appear as if a drop of dew hung at their tails which had been set on fire by the fairys for the purpose of a lanthorn—and I have often gathered them up and put them into leaves to see if they shone by daylight but when day came they were nothing but a little dark looking insect apparently half dead and as it were shrivelled up another insect is as commonly and infact more commonly known as the gloworm among the common people because it frequents their houses shining very brilliantly anights like liquid silver and leaving if touchd part of its shining qualities littered about where it crawled   this when seen by day light is a red long insect with a great quantity of legs and therebye called the forty legged worm

The Nightingales Nest

UP this green woodland ride lets softly rove
And list the nightingale—she dwelleth here
Hush let the wood gate softly clap—for fear
The noise may drive her from her home of love
For here Ive heard her many a merry year
At morn and eve nay all the live long day
As though she lived on song—this very spot
Just where that old mans beard all wildly trails
Rude arbours oer the road and stops the way
And where that child its blue bell flowers hath got
Laughing and creeping through the mossy rails
There have I hunted like a very boy
Creeping on hands and knees through matted thorns
To find her nest and see her feed her young
And vainly did I many hours employ
All seemed as hidden as a thought unborn
And where these crimping* fern leaves ramp* among
The hazels under boughs—Ive nestled down
And watched her while she sung—and her renown
Hath made me marvel that so famed a bird
Should have no better dress than russet brown
Her wings would tremble in her extacy
And feathers stand on end as twere with joy
And mouth wide open to release her heart
Of its out sobbing songs—the happiest part
Of summers fame she shared—for so to me
Did happy fancys shapen her employ
But if I touched a bush or scarcely stirred
All in a moment stopt—I watched in vain

The timid bird had left the hazel bush
And at a distance hid to sing again
Lost in a wilderness of listening leaves
Rich extacy would pour its luscious strain
Till envy spurred the emulating thrush
To start less wild and scarce inferior songs
For cares with him for half the year remain
To damp the ardour of his speckled breast
While nightingales to summers life belongs
And naked trees and winters nipping wrongs
Are strangers to her music and her rest
Her joys are evergreen her world is wide
—Hark there she is as usual lets be hush
For in this black thorn clump if rightly guest
Her curious house is hidden—part aside
These hazel branches in a gentle way
And stoop right cautious neath the rustling boughs
For we will have another search to-day
And hunt this fern strown thorn clump round and round
And where this seeded wood grass idly bows
Well wade right through—it is a likely nook
In such like spots and often on the ground
Theyll build where rude boys never think to look
Aye as I live her secret nest is here
Upon this white thorn stulp—Ive searched about
For hours in vain—there put that bramble bye
Nay trample on its branches and get near
—How subtle is the bird she started out
And raised a plaintive note of danger nigh
Ere we were past the brambles and now near
Her nest she sudden stops—as choking fear
That might betray her home so even now
Well leave it as we found it—safetys guard
Of pathless solitude shall keep it still
See there shes sitting on the old oak bough
Mute in her fears our presence doth retard
Her joys and doubt turns all her rapture chill

   Sing on sweet bird may no worse hap befall
Thy visions then the fear that now decieves

We will not plunder music of its dower
Nor turn this spot of happiness to thrall
For melody seems hid in every flower
That blossoms near thy home—these harebells all
Seems bowing with the beautiful in song
And gaping cuckoo with its spotted leaves
Seems blushing of the singing it has heard
How curious is the nest no other bird
Uses such loose materials or weaves
Their dwellings in such spots—dead oaken leaves
Are placed without and velvet moss within
And little scraps of grass—and scant and spare
Of what seems scarce materials down and hair
For from mans haunts she seemeth nought to win
Yet nature is the builder and contrives
Homes for her childerns comfort even here
Where solitudes deciples spend their lives
Unseen save when a wanderer passes near
That loves such pleasant places—deep adown
The nest is made an hermits mossy cell
Snug lie her curious eggs in number five
Of deadened green or rather olive brown
And the old prickly thorn bush guards them well
And here well leave them still unknown to wrong
As the old woodlands legacy of song

April 21 [1825]

I WENT to take my walk to day and heard the Nightingale for the
first time this season in Royce wood just at the town end   we may
now be assured that the summer is nigh at hand you asked me a long
while back to procure you a Nightingales nest and eggs and I have
try'd every season since to find if the bird nesting boys have ever
taken one out but I have not been able to procure one—when I was
a boy I usd to be very curious to watch the nightingale to find her
nest and to observe her color and size for I had heard many odd tales
about her and I often observed her habits and found her nest so I
shall be able to give you a pretty faithful history—she is a plain bird

somthing like the hedge sparrow in shape and the female Firetail or Redstart in color but more slender then the former and of a redder brown or scorchd color then the latter   the breast of the male or female is spotted like a young Robin and the feathers on the rump and on parts of the wings are of a fox red or burnt umber hue   one of them is of a darker brown then the other but I know not wether it be the male or female   they generally seek the same solitudes which they haunted last season and these are the black thorn clumps and thickets about the woods and spinneys   they sit in the water grains* of oaks or on a twig of hazel and sing their varied songs with short intervals both in the night and day time and sing in one as common as the other   I have watchd them often at their song   their mouths is open very wide and their feathers are ruffled up and their wings trembling as if in extacy   the superstition of laying their throats on a sharp thorn is a foolish absurdity but it is not the only one ascribed to the nightingale   they make a large nest of the old oak leaves that strew the ground in woods and green moss and line it with hair and some times a little fine witherd grass or whool   it is a very deep nest and is generaly placed on the root or stulp of a black or white thorn somtimes a little height up the bush and often on the ground

they lay 5 eggs about the size of the woodlarks or larger and of a deep olive brown without spot or tinge of another color   their eggs have a very odd appearance and are unlike any other birds in the county   when they have young their song ceases and they make an odd burring noise as if calling their young to their food   they are very jealous of intrusions on their privacy when they have young and if one goes in their haunts at that time they make a great chirping and burring and will almost perch close to you noising and chirping as if to fight you away   at first one assails you and after it has been chirping about you a while the other approaches to join it but as soon as you get a little distance from the haunts they leave you and are still   when if you return they resume their former chirping and continue fluttering about you among the branches till you leave them agen to their privacy

their nest[s] are very difficult to find   indeed it is a hopless task to hunt for them as they are seldom found but by accident being hidden among the tall weeds that surround the roots and cover the woods undisturbed recesses   when I was a boy I found three nests one season and all were found by chance in crossing the woods hunting the

nests of other birds—the Red breast frequently builds on the ground
under the shelter of a knoll or stulp and its nest is often taken for that
of the nightingales but it is easily distinguished from it as the robins
is built with dead grass and moss on the out side while the Nightingale never forgets her dead oak leaves and this is so peculiar to her
taste that I never saw a nest of theirs without them nor are they used
by any other bird for their nests—

ᴐᴐᴐᴐᴐ

The Sky Lark

THE rolls and harrows lies at rest beside
The battered road and spreading far and wide
Above the russet clods the corn is seen
Sprouting its spirey points of tender green
Where squats the hare to terrors wide awake
Like some brown clod the harrows failed to break
While neath the warm hedge boys stray far from home
To crop the early blossoms as they come
Where buttercups will make them eager run
Opening their golden caskets to the sun
To see who shall be first to pluck the prize
And from their hurry up the sky lark flies
And oer her half formed nest with happy wings
Winnows* the air till in the clouds she sings
Then hangs a dust spot in the sunny skies
And drops and drops till in her nest she lies
Where boys unheeding past—neer dreaming then
That birds which flew so high would drop agen
To nests upon the ground where any thing
May come at to destroy had they the wing
Like such a bird themselves would be too proud
And build on nothing but a passing cloud
As free from danger as the heavens are free
From pain and toil—there would they build and be
And sail about the world to scenes unheard
Of and unseen—O where they but a bird

So think they while they listen to its song
And smile and fancy and so pass along
While its low nest moist with the dews of morn
Lies safely with the leveret in the corn

The Ravens Nest

UPON the collar of an hugh* old oak
Year after year boys mark a curious nest
Of twigs made up a faggot near in size
And boys to reach it try all sorts of schemes
But not a twig to reach with hand or foot
Sprouts from the pillared trunk and as to try
To swarm the massy bulk tis all in vain
They scarce one effort make to hitch them up
But down they sluther* soon as ere they try
So long hath been their dwelling there—old men
When passing bye will laugh and tell the ways
They had when boys to climb that very tree
And as it so would seem that very nest
That ne'er was missing from that self same spot
A single year in all their memorys
And they will say that the two birds are now
The very birds that owned the dwelling then
Some think it strange yet certaintys at loss
And cannot contradict it so they pass
As old birds living the woods patriarchs
Old as the oldest men so famed and known
That even men will thirst into the fame
Of boys at get at schemes that now and then
May captivate a young one from the tree
With iron claums* and bands adventuring up
The mealy trunk or else by waggon ropes
Slung over the hugh grains and so drawn up
By those at bottom one assends secure
With foot rope stirruped—still a perrilous way
So perrilous that one and only one
In memorys of the oldest men was known

78

To wear* his boldness to intentions end
And reach the ravens nest—and thence acchieved
A theme that wonder treasured for supprise
By every cottage hearth the village through
Not yet forgot though other darers come
With daring times that scale the steeples top
And tye their kerchiefs to the weather cock
As trophys that the dangerous deed was done
Yet even now in these adventureous days
No one is bold enough to dare the way
Up the old monstrous oak where every spring
Finds the two ancient birds at their old task
Repairing the hugh nest—where still they live
Through changes winds and storms and are secure
And like a landmark in the chronicles
Of village memorys treasured up yet lives
The hugh old oak that wears the ravens nest

The Moorehens Nest

O POESYS power thou overpowering sweet
That renders hearts that love thee all unmeet
For this rude world its trouble and its care
Loading the heart with joys it cannot bear
That warms and chills and burns and bursts at last
Oer broken hopes and troubles never past
I pay thee worship at a rustic shrine
And dream oer joys I still imagine mine
I pick up flowers and pebbles and by thee
As gems and jewels they appear to me
I pick out pictures round the fields that lie
In my minds heart like things that cannot die
Like picking hopes and making friends with all
Yet glass will often bear a harder fall
As bursting bottles loose the precious wine
Hopes casket breaks and I the gems resign
Pain shadows on till feelings self decays
And all such pleasures leave me is their praise

And thus each fairy vision melts away
Like evening landscapes from the face of day
Till hope returns with aprils dewy reign
And then I start and seek for joy again
And pick her fragments up to hurd anew
Like fancy riches pleasure loves to view
And these associations of the past
Like summer pictures in a winter blast
Renews my heart to feelings as the rain
Falls on the earth and bids it thrive again
Then een the fallow fields appear so fair
The very weeds make sweetest gardens there
And summer there puts garments on so gay
I hate the plough that comes to dissaray
Her holiday delights—and labours toil
Seems vulgar curses on the sunny soil
And man the only object that distrains
Earths garden into deserts for his gains
Leave him his schemes of gain—tis wealth to me
Wild heaths to trace—and note their broken tree
Which lightening shivered—and which nature tries
To keep alive for poesy to prize
Upon whose mossy roots my leisure sits
To hear the birds pipe oer their amorous fits
Though less beloved for singing then the taste
They have to choose such homes upon the waste
Rich architects—and then the spots to see
How picturesque their dwelling makes them be
The wild romances of the poets mind
No sweeter pictures for their tales can find
And so I glad my heart and rove along
Now finding nests—then listening to a song
Then drinking fragrance whose perfuming cheats
Tinges lifes sours and bitters into sweets
That heart stirred fragrance when the summers rain
Lays the roads dust and sprouts the grass again
Filling the cracks up on the beaten paths
And breathing insence from the mowers swaths
Insence the bards and prophets of old days

Met in the wilderness to glad their praise
And in these summer walks I seem to feel
These bible pictures in their essence steal
Around me—and the ancientness of joy
Breath from the woods till pleasures even cloy
Yet holy breathing manna seemly falls
With angel answers if a trouble calls
And then I walk and swing my stick for joy
And catch at little pictures passing bye
A gate whose posts are two old dotterel trees
A close with molehills sprinkled oer its leas
A little footbrig with its crossing rail
A wood gap stopt with ivy wreathing pale
A crooked stile each path crossed spinney owns
A brooklet forded by its stepping stones
A wood bank mined with rabbit holes—and then
An old oak leaning oer a badgers den
Whose cave mouth enters neath the twisted charms
Of its old roots and keeps it safe from harms
Pick axes spades and all its strength confounds
When hunted foxes hide from chasing hounds—
Then comes the meadows where I love to see
A flood washed bank support an aged tree
Whose roots are bare—yet some with foothold good
Crankle* and spread and strike beneath the flood
Yet still it leans as safer hold to win
On tother side and seems as tumbling in
While every summer finds it green and gay
And winter leaves it safe as did the may
Nor does the More hen find its safety vain
For on its roots their last years homes remain
And once again a couple from the brood
Seek their old birth place—and in safetys mood
Lodge there their flags and lay—though danger comes
It dares and tries and cannot reach their homes
And so they hatch their eggs and sweetly dream
On their shelfed nests that bridge the gulphy stream
And soon the sutty brood from fear elopes
Where bulrush forrests give them sweeter hopes

81

Their hanging nest that aids their wishes well
Each leaves for water as it leaves the shell
And dive and dare and every gambol try
Till they themselves to other scenes can fly

Pewits Nest

ACCROSS the fallow clods at early morn
I took a random track where scant and spare
The grass and nibbled leaves all closely shorn
Leaves a burnt flat all bleaching brown and bare
Where hungry sheep in freedom range forlorn
And neath the leaning willow and odd thorn
And molehill large that vagrant shade supplies
They batter round to shun the teazing flies
Trampling smooth places hard as cottage floors
Where the time killing lonely shepherd boys
Whose summer homes are ever out of doors
Their chock holes form and chalk their marble ring
And make their clay taws at the bubbling spring
And in their wrangling sport and gambling joys
They strime* their clock like shadows—when it cloys
To guess the hour that slowly runs away
And shorten sultry turmoil with their play

Here did I roam while veering over nead
The pewet whirred in many whewing rings
And 'chewsit' screamed and clapped her flopping wings
To hunt her nest my rambling steps was led
Oer the broad baulk beset with little hills
By moles long formed and pismires tennanted
As likely spots but still I searched in vain
When all at once the noisey birds were still
And on the lands a furrowed ridge between
Chance found four eggs of dingy olive green
Deep blotched with plashy spots of jockolate* stain

Their small ends inward turned as ever found
As though some curious hand had laid them round
Yet lying on the ground with nought at all
Of soft grass withered twitch and bleached weed
To keep them from the rain storms frequent fall
And here she broods on her unsavoury bed
When bye and bye with little care and heed
Her young with each a shell upon its head
Run after their wild parents restless cry
And from their own fears tiney shadows run
Neath clods and stones to cringe and snugly lie
Hid from all sight but the allseeing sun
Till never ceasing danger seemeth bye

Crows in Spring

THE crow will tumble up and down
　　At the first sight of spring
And in old trees around the town
　　Brush winter from its wing

No longer flapping far away
　　To naked fen they flye
Chill fare as on a winters day
　　But field and valleys nigh

Where swains are stirring out to plough
　　And woods are just at hand
They seek the uplands sunny brow
　　And strut from land to land

And often flap their sooty wings
　　And sturt to neighboring tree
And seems to try all ways to sing
　　And almost speaks in glee

The ploughman hears and turns his head
　　Above to wonder why
And there a new nest nearly made
　　Proclaims the winter bye

The schoolboy free from winters frown
    That rests on every stile
In wonder sets his basket down
    To start his happy toil

Insects

THOU tiney loiterer on the barleys beard
And happy unit of a numerous herd
Of playfellows the laughing summer brings
Mocking the suns face in their glittering wings
How merrily they creep and run and flye
No kin they bear to labours drudgery
Smoothing the velvet of the pale hedge rose
And where they flye for dinner no one knows
The dewdrops feed them not—they love the shine
Of noon whose sun may bring them golden wine
All day theyre playing in their sunday dress
Till night goes sleep and they can do no less
Then in the heath bells silken hood they flie
And like to princes in their slumber lie
From coming night and dropping dews and all
In silken beds and roomy painted hall
So happily they spend their summer day
Now in the corn fields now the new mown hay
One almost fancys that such happy things
In coloured moods and richly burnished wings
Are fairey folk in splendid masquerade
Disguised through fear of mortal folk affraid
Keeping their merry pranks a mystery still
Lest glaring day should do their secrets ill

[The Badger]

THE badger grunting on his woodland track
With shaggy hide and sharp nose scrowed* with black
Roots in the bushes and the woods and makes
A great hugh burrow in the ferns and brakes

With nose on ground he runs a awkard pace
And anything will beat him in the race
The shepherds dog will run him to his den
Followed and hooted by the dogs and men
The woodman when the hunting comes about
Go round at night to stop the foxes out
And hurrying through the bushes ferns and brakes
Nor sees the many hol[e]s the badger makes
And often through the bushes to the chin
Breaks the old holes and tumbles headlong in

When midnight comes a host of dogs and men
Go out and track the badger to his den
And put a sack within the hole and lye
Till the old grunting badger passes bye
He comes and hears they let the strongest loose
The old fox hears the noise and drops the goose
The poacher shoots and hurrys from the cry
And the old hare half wounded buzzes bye
They get a forked stick to bear him down
And clapt the dogs and bore him to the town
And bait him all the day with many dogs
And laugh and shout and fright the scampering hogs
He runs along and bites at all he meets
They shout and hollo down the noisey streets

He turns about to face the loud uproar
And drives the rebels to their very doors
The frequent stone is hurled where ere they go
When badgers fight and every ones a foe
The dogs are clapt and urged to join the fray
The badger turns and drives them all away
Though scarcly half as big dimute* and small
He fights with dogs for hours and beats them all
The heavy mastiff savage in the fray
Lies down and licks his feet and turns away
The bull dog knows his match and waxes cold
The badger grins and never leaves his hold
He drive[s] the crowd and follows at their heels
And bites them through the drunkard swears and reels

The frighted women takes the boys away
The blackguard laughs and hurrys on the fray
He tries to reach the woods a awkard race
But sticks and cudgels quickly stop the chace
He turns agen and drives the noisey crowd
And beats the many dogs in noises loud
He drives away and beats them every one
And then they loose them all and set them on
He falls as dead and kicked by boys and men
Then starts and grins and drives the crowd agen
Till kicked and torn and beaten out he lies
And leaves his hold and cackles groans and dies

Some keep a baited badger tame as hog
And tame him till he follows like the dog
They urge him on like dogs and show fair play
He beats and scarcely wounded goes away
Lapt up as if asleep he scorns to fly
And siezes any dog that ventures nigh
Clapt like a dog he never bites the men
But worrys dogs and hurrys to his den
They let him out and turn a harrow down
And there he fights the host of all the town
He licks the patting hand and trys to play
And never trys to bite or run away
And runs away from noise in hollow trees
Burnt by the boys to get a swarm of bees

[*The Marten*]

THE martin cat long shaged of courage good
Of weazle shape a dweller in the wood
With badger hair long shagged and darting eyes
And lower then the common cat in size
Small head and running on the stoop
Snuffing the ground and hind parts shouldered up
He keeps one track and hides in lonely shade
Where print of human foot is scarcely made

Save when the woods are cut the beaten track
The woodmans dog will snuff cock tailed and black
Red legged and spotted over either eye
Snuffs barks and scrats the lice and passes bye
The great brown horned owl looks down below
And sees the shaggy martin come and go

The martin hurrys through the woodland gaps
And poachers shoot and make his skin for caps
When any woodman come and pass the place
He looks at dogs and scarcely mends his pace
And gipseys often and birdnesting boys
Look in the hole and hear a hissing noise
They climb the tree such noise they never heard
And think the great owl is a foreign bird
When the grey owl her young ones cloathed in down
Seizes the boldest boy and drives him down
They try agen and pelt* to start the fray
The grey owl comes and drives them all away
And leaves the martin twisting round his den
Left free from boys and dogs and noise and men

[*The Fox*]

THE shepherd on his journey heard when nigh
His dog among the bushes barking high
The ploughman ran and gave a hearty shout
He found a weary fox and beat him out
The ploughman laughed and would have ploughed him in
But the old shepherd took him for the skin
He lay upon the furrow stretched and dead
The old dog lay and licked the wounds that bled
The ploughman beat him till his ribs would crack
And then the shepherd slung him at his back
And when he rested to his dogs supprise
The old fox started from his dead disguise
And while the dog lay panting in the sedge
He up and snapt and bolted through the hedge

He scampered [to] the bushes far away
The shepherd call[ed] the ploughman [to] the fray
The ploughman wished he had a gun to shoot
The old dog barked and followed the pursuit
The shepherd through [sic] his hook and tottered past
The ploughman ran but none could go so fast
The woodman threw his faggot from the way
And ceased to chop and wondered at the fray
But when he saw the dog and heard the cry
He threw his hatchet but the fox was bye
The shepherd broke his hook and lost the skin
He found a badger hole and bolted in
They tryed to dig but safe from dangers way
He lived to chase the hounds another day

[The Hedgehog]

THE hedgehog hides beneath the rotten hedge
And makes a great round nest of grass and sedge
Or in a bush or in a hollow tree
And many often stoops and say they see
Him roll and fill his prickles full of crab[s]*
And creep away and where the magpie dabs*
His wing at muddy dyke in aged root
He makes a nest and fills it full of fruit
On the hedge bottom hunts for crabs and sloes
And whistles like a cricket as he goes
It rolls up like a ball or shapeless hog
When gipseys hunt it with their noisey dogs
Ive seen it in their camps they call it sweet
Though black and bitter and unsavoury meat

But they who hunt the field for rotten meat
And wash in muddy dyke and call it sweat [sic]
And eat what dogs refuse where ere they dwell
Care little either for the taste or smell
They say they milk the cows and when they lye
Nibble their fleshy teats and make them dry

88

But they whove seen the small head like a hog
Rolled up to meet the savage of a dog
With mouth scarce big enough to hold a straw
Will neer believe what no one ever saw
But still they hunt the hedges all about
And shepherd dogs are trained to hunt them out
They hurl with savage force the stick and stone
And no one cares and still the strife goes on

Hares at Play

THE birds are gone to bed the cows are still
And sheep lie panting on each old mole hill
And underneath the willows grey green bough
Like toil a resting—lies the fallow plough
The timid hares throw daylights fears away
On the lanes road to dust and dance and play
Then dabble in the grain by nought deterred
To lick the dewfall from the barleys beard
Then out they sturt again and round the hill
Like happy thoughts dance squat and loiter still
Till milking maidens in the early morn
Gingle their yokes and start them in the corn
Through well known beaten paths each nimbling hare
Sturts quick as fear—and seeks its hidden lair

The Robin

AGAIN the robin waxes tame
And ventures pitys crumbs to claim
Picking the trifles off the snow
Which dames on purpose daily throw
And perching on the window sill
Where memory recolecting still
Knows the last winters broken pane
And there he hops and peeps again

THE little Robin has begun his summer song in good earnest   he was singing at my chamber window this morning almost before daylight as he has done all the week and at night fall he comes regularly to his old plumb tree and starts it again   there is a plaintive sweetness in the song of this bird that I am very fond of   it may be calld an eternal song for it is heard at intervals all the year round and in the Autumn when the leaves are all fled from the trees there is a mellancholy sweetness in it that is very touching to my feelings   the Robin is one of the most familiar birds that a village landscape posseses and it is no less beloved for even childern leave its nest unmolested but the Wren and the Martin are held in the like veneration with a many people who will not suffer their nests to be destroyed   the Robin seems to be fond of the company and haunts of man   it builds its nest close to his cottage in the hovel or out house thatch or behind the woodbine or sweet briar in the garden wall nor does it seem to care to make any secret of its dwelling were its only enemy is the cat to whom its confidence of saftey often falls a prey   and it seeks its food by his door on the dunghill or on the garden beds   nay it will even settle on the gardeners spade when he is at work to watch the worm that he throws up and unbears and in winter it will venture into the house for food and become as tame as a chicken   we had one that usd to come in at a broken pane in the window three winters together   I always knew it to be our old visitor by a white scar on one of the wings which might have been an old wound made by some cat   it grew so tame that it woud perch on ones finger and take the crumbs out of the hand   it was very much startled at the cat at first but after a time it took little notice of her further then always contriving to keep out of her way   it woud never stay in the house at night tho it woud attempt to perch on the chair spindles and clean its bill and ruffle its feathers and put its head under its wing as if it had made up its mind to stay but somthing or other always molested it when it suddenly sought its old broken pane and departed . . . it has been a common notion among heedless observers that the robin frequents no were but in villages but this is an erronious one for it is found in the deepest solitudes of woods and forrests were it lives on insects and builds its nest on the roots or stools* of the underwood or under a hanging bank by a dykeside which is often mistook for that of the nightingales   I have often observed its fondness for man even here for in summer I scarcely cross a wood but a Robin suddenly falls in

my path to court my acquaintance and pay me a visit were it hops
and flutters about as if pleased to see me and in winter it is the woodmans companion for the whole day and the whole season . . . It is not
commonly known that the Robin is a very quarrelsome bird   it is not
only at frequent warfare with its own species but attacks boldly every
other small bird that comes in its way and is gennerally the conqeror
I have seen it chase the house sparrow which tho a very pert bird
never ventures to fight it   hedge sparrows linnets and finches that
crowd the barn doors in winter never stands against its authority but
flyes from its interferences and acknowledge it the cock of the walk
and he always seems to consider the right of the yard as his own

◡◠◡◠◡◠

The Robins Nest

COME luscious spring come with thy mossy roots
Thy weed strown banks—young grass—and tender shoots
Of woods new plashed sweet smells of opening blooms
Sweet sunny mornings and right glorious dooms
Of happiness—to seek and harbour in
Far from the ruder worlds inglorious din
Who sees no glory but in sordid pelf
And nought of greatness but its little self
Scorning the splendid gift that nature gives
Where natures glory ever breaths and lives
Seated in crimping* ferns uncurling now
In russet fringes ere in leaves they bow
And moss as green as silk—there let me be
By the grey powdered trunk of old oak tree
Buried in green delights to which the heart
Clings with delight and beats as loath to part
The birds unbid come round about and give
Their music to my pleasures—wild flowers live
About as if for me—they smile and bloom
Like uninvited guests that love to come
Their wildwood fragrant offerings all to bring
Paying me kindness like a throned king
Lost in such extacys in this old spot

91

I feel that rapture which the world hath not
That joy like health that flushes in my face
Amid the brambles of this ancient place
Shut out from all but that superior power
That guards and glads and cheers me every hour
That wraps me like a mantle from the storm
Of care and bids the coldest hope be warm
That speaks in spots where all things silent be
In words not heard but felt—each ancient tree
With lickens deckt—times hoary pedigree
Becomes a monitor to teach and bless
And rid me of the evils cares possess
And bid me look above the trivial things
To which prides mercenary spirit clings
The pomps the wealth and artificial toys
That men call wealth beleagued with strife and noise
To seek the silence of their ancient reign
And be myself in memory once again
To trace the paths of briar entangled holt
Or bushy closen where the wanton colt
Crops the young juicey leaves from off the hedge
In this old wood where birds their passions pledge
And court and build and sing their undersong
In joys own cue that to their hearts belong
Having no wish or want unreconsiled
But spell bound to their homes within the wild
Where old neglect lives patron and befriends
Their homes with safetys wildness—where nought lends
A hand to injure—root up or disturb
The things of this old place—there is no curb
Of interest industry or slavish gain
To war with nature so the weeds remain
And wear an ancient passion that arrays
Ones feelings with the shadows of old days
The rest of peace the sacredness of mind
In such deep solitudes we seek and find
Where moss grows old and keeps an evergreen
And footmarks seem like miracles when seen
So little meddling toil doth trouble here

The very weeds as patriarchs appear
And if a plant ones curious eyes delight
In this old ancient solitude we might
Come ten years hence of trouble dreaming ill
And find them like old tennants peaceful still
Here the wood robin rustling on the leaves
With fluttering step each visitor recieves
Yet from his ancient home he seldom stirs
In heart content on these dead teazle burs
He sits and trembles oer his under notes
So rich—joy almost chokes his little throat
With extacy and from his own heart flows
That joy himself and partner only knows
He seems to have small fear but hops and comes
Close to ones feet as if he looked for crumbs
And when the woodman strinkles* some around
He leaves the twig and hops upon the ground
And feeds untill his little daintys cloy
Then shakes his little wings and sings for joy
    And when in woodland solitudes I wend
I always hail him as my hermit friend
And naturally enough whenere they come
Before me search my pockets for a crumb
At which he turns his eye and seems to stand
As if expecting somthing from my hand
And thus these feathered heirs of solitude
Remain the tennants of this quiet wood
And live in melody and make their home
And never seem to have a wish to roam
Beside this ash stulp where in years gone bye
The thrush had built and taught her young to flye
Where still the nest half filled with leaves remains
With moss still green amid the twisting grains
Here on the ground and sheltered at its foot
The nest is hid close at its mossy root
Composed of moss and grass and lined with hair
And five brun-coloured* eggs snug sheltered there
And bye and bye a happy brood will be
The tennants of this woodland privacy

A Sunday with Shepherds and Herdboys

THE shepherds and the herding swains
Keep their sabbath on the plains
They know no difference in its cares
Save that all toil has ceasd but theirs
For them the church bells vainly call
Fields are their church and house and all
Till night returns their homward track
When soon morns suns recall them back
Yet still they love the days repose
And feel its peace as sweet as those
That have their freedom—and maid and clown
To walk the meadows or the town
Theyll lye and catch the humming sound
That comes from steeples shining round
Enjoying in the service time
The happy bells delightfull chime
And oft they sit on rising ground
To view the landscap spreading round
Swimming from the following eye
In greens and stems of every dye
Oer wood and vale and fens smooth lap
Like a richly colourd map
Square platts* of clover red and white
Scented wi summers warm delight
And sinkfoil* of a fresher stain
And different greens of varied grain
Wheat spindles bursted into ear
And browning faintly—grasses sere
In swathy seed pods dryd by heat
Rustling when brushd by passing feet
And beans and peas of deadening green
And corn lands ribbon stripes between
And checkering* villages that lye
Like light spots in a deeper sky
And woods black greens that crowding spots
The lanscape in leaf bearing grots
Were mingling hid lapt up to lare*

The panting fox lyes cooly there
And willow grove that idly sweas*
And checkering shines mid other trees
As if the mornings misty vail
Yet lingerd in their shadows pale
While from the village foliage pops
The popples* tapering to their tops
That in the blue sky thinly wires
Like so many leafy spires
Thus the shepherd as he lyes
Were the heaths furze swellings rise
Dreams oer the scene in visions sweet
Stretching from his hawthorn seat
And passes many an hour away
Thus musing on the sabbath day
And from the fields theyll often steal
The green peas for a sunday meal
When near* a farmers on the lurch
Safe nodding oer their books a church*
Or on their benches by the door
Telling their market profits oer
And in snug nooks their huts beside
The gipsey blazes they provide
Braking the rotten* from the trees
While some sit round to shell the peas
Or pick from hedges pilferd wood
To boil on props their stolen food
Sitting on stones or heaps of brakes*
Each of the wild repast partakes
Telling to pass the hours along
Tales that to fitter days belong
While one within his scrip* contains
A shatterd bibles thumbd remains
On whose blank leaf wi pious care
A host of names is scribbld there
Names by whom twas once possest
Or those in kindred bonds carresst
Childern for generations back
That doubtful memory should not lack

Their dates tis there wi care applyd
When they were born and when they dyd
From sire to son link after link
All scribbld wi unsparing ink
This he will oft pull out and read
That takes of sunday better heed
Then they who laugh at tale and jest
And oft hell read it to the rest
Whose ignorance in weary mood
Pays more regard to robin hood
And giant blue beard and such tales
That live like flowers in rural vales
Natural as last years faded blooms
Anew wi the fresh season comes
So these old tales from old to young
Take root and blossom were they sprung
Till age and winter bids them wane
Then fond youth takes them up again
The herdboys anxious after play
Find sports to pass the time away
Fishing for struttles* in the brooks
Wi thread for lines and pins for hooks
And stripping neath the willow shade
In warm and muddy ponds to bathe
And pelting wi unerring eye
The heedless swallows starting bye
Oft breaking boughs from trees to kill
The nest of whasps beside a hill
Till one gets stung then they resort
And follow to less dangerous sport
Leaving to chance their sheep and cows
To thread the brakes and forest boughs
And scare the squirrels lively joys
Wi stones and sticks and shouting noise
That sat wi in its secret place
Upon its tale to clean its face
When found they shout wi joy to see
It hurly burly round a tree
And as they turn in sight again

It peeps and squats behind a grain
And oft theyll cut up sticks to trye
The holes were badgers darkly lye
Looking for foot mark prints about
The fresh moulds not long rooted out
And peep in burroes newly done
Were rabbits from their noses run
Were oft in terrors wild affright
They spy and startle at the sight
Rolld like a whip thong round and round
Asleep upon the sunny ground
A snake that wakens at their play
And starts as full of fear as they
And knewt* shapd swifts that nimbly pass
And rustle in the brown heath grass
From these in terrors fears they haste
And seek agen the scrubby waste
Were grass is pincered short by sheep
And venom creatures rarely creep
Playing at taw in sheep beat tracks
Or leap frog oer each others backs
Or hump oer hills wi thime oergrown
Or mere marks ancient mossey stone
Or run down hollows in the plain
Were steps are cut to climb again
Stone pits that years have clothd in green
And slopd in narrow vales between
Or historys uncrowded ground
A cromwell trench or roman mound
Thus will the boys wi makeshift joy
Their toil taskd sabbath hours employ
And feed on fancys sweet as they
That in the town at freedom play
And pinder* too is peeping round
To find a tennant for his pound
Heedless of rest or parsons prayers
He seldom to the church repairs
But thinks religion hath its due
In paying yearly for his pew

Soon as the morn puts night away
And hastening on her mantle grey
Before one sunbeam oer the ground
Spindles its light and shadow round
He's oer the fields as soon as morn
To see what stock are in the corn
And find what chances sheep may win
Thro gaps the gipseys pilfer thin
Or if theyve found a restless way
By rubbing at a loosend tray*
Or neighing colt that trys to catch
A gate at night left off the latch
By traveller seeking home in haste
Or the clown by fancys chasd
That lasting while he made a stand
Opens each gate wi fearful hand
Fearing a minute to remain
And put it on the latch again
And cows who often wi their horns
Toss from the gaps the stuffing thorns
These like a fox upon the watch
He in the morning tryes to catch
And drives them to the pound for pay
Carless about the sabbath day

The Shepherds Fire

ON the rude heath yclad in furze and ling
And oddling thorns that thick and prickly grows
Shielding the shepherd when the rude wind blows
And boys that sit right merry in a ring
Round fires upon a molehill toasting sloes
And crabs that froth and frizzle on the coals
Loud is the gabble and the laughter loud
The rabbits scarce dare peep from out their holes
Unwont to mix with such a noisey crowd
Some run to eke the fire—while many a cloud

Of smoke curls up some on their haunches squat
With mouth for bellows puffing till it flares
Or if that fail one fans his napless hat
And when the feast is done they squabble for their shares

Shepherds Hut

THE shepherds hut propt by the double ash
Hugh in its bulk and old in mossy age
Shadowing the dammed up brook where plash and plash
The little mills did younkers ears engage
Delightful hut rude as romances old
Where hugh old stones make each an easy chair
And brakes and ferns for luxurys manifold
And flint and steel the all want needeth there
—The light was struck and then the happy ring
Crouched round the blaze—O these were happy times
Some telling tales and others urged to sing
Themes of old things in rude yet feeling ryhmes
That raised the laugh and stirred the stifled sigh
Till pity listened in each vacant eye

Those rude old tales—mans memory augurs ill
Thus to forget the fragments of old days
Those long old songs—their sweetness haunts me still
Nor did they perish for my lack of praise
But old desciples of the pasture sward
Rude chronicles of ancient minstrelsy
The shepherds vanished all and disregard
Left their old music like a vagrant bee
For summers breeze to murmur oer and die
And in these ancient spots mind ear and eye
Turn listeners—till the very wind prolongs
The theme as wishing in its depths of joy
To reccolect the music of old songs
And meet the hut that blessed me when a boy

I WAS fond of books before I began to write poetry   these were such that chance came at—6py Pamphlets that are in the possesion of every door calling hawker and found on every book stall at fairs and markets whose titles are as familiar with every one as his own name   shall I repeat some of them   'Little red riding hood' 'Valentine and Orson' 'Jack and the Jiant' 'Tom Long the carrier' 'The king and the cobler' 'Sawney Bear' 'The seven Sleepers' 'Tom Hickathrift' 'Johnny Armstrong' 'Idle Laurence'. . . 'Robin Hoods garland' 'old mother Shipton and old Nixons Prophecys' 'History of Gotham' and many others   shall I go on   no these have memorys as common as Prayer Books and Psalters with the peasantry   such were the books that delighted me and I savd all the pence I got to buy them for they were the whole world of literature to me and I knew of no other   I carried them in my pocket and read them at my leisure and they was the never weary food of winter evenings ere Milton Shakspear and Thompson had ever existed in my memory and I feel a love for them still   nay I cannot help fancying now that cock robin babes in the wood mother hubbard and her cat etc etc are real poetry in all its native simplicity and as it shoud be   I know I am foolish enough to have fancys different from others and childhood is a strong spell over my feelings but I think so on and cannot help it

PLEASURES are of two kinds   one arises from cultivation of the mind and are enjoyed only by the few and these are the most lasting and least liable to change   the more common pleasures are found by the many like beautiful weeds in a wilderness   they are of natural growth and tho very beautiful to the eye are only annuals   these may be called the pleasures of the passions and belong only to the different stages of our existance   the pleasures of youth are enjoyd in youth only   after that the very reccolections of their sweetness sour and embitter the infirmitys of manhood that can no longer enjoy them

⁕⁕⁕⁕⁕

[*What is there in the distant hills*]

WHAT is there in the distant hills
My fancy longs to see
That many a mood of joy instills
Say what can fancy be

Do old oaks thicken all the woods
With weeds and brakes as here
Does common water make the floods
Thats common every where

Is grass the green that cloaths the ground
Are springs the common spring
Daisy and cowslap dropping round
Are such the flowers she brings

Their brooms are they the yellow broom
Their briers the smelling brier
Questions from fancy seldom come
But such are evry where

Does day come with its common sky
Thats seen both near and far
Does night the selfsame moon supply
With many a little star

Are cottages of mud and stone
By vally wood and glen
And their calm dwellers little known
Men and but common men

That drive afield with cart and plough
Such men are common here
And pastoral maidens milking cows
Dwell almost every where

If so my fancy idly clings
To notions far away
And longs to roam for common things
All round her every day

Right idle would the journey be
To leave ones home so far
And see the moon I now can see
And every little star

And have they there a night and day
And common counted hours
And do they see so far away
This very moon of ours

That seems to fill a little round
In shining up and down
As if like stars enow were found
To shine for every town

I mark him climb above the trees
With one small couzin star
And think me in my reveries
He cannot shine so far

And on his face that ancient man
Will ever stooping be
What else he is no sort of plan
Could ever get to see

The poets in the tales they tell
And with their happy powers
Have made lands where their fancys dwell
Seem better lands then ours

Their storied woods and vales and streams
Grow up within the mind
Like beauty seen in pleasant dreams
We no where else can find

Yet common things no matter what
Which nature dignifyes
If happ[i]ness be in their lot
They gratify our eyes

Some value things from being new
Yet nature keeps the old
She watches oer the humblest too
In blessings manifold

The common things of every day
However mean or small
The heedless eye may throw away
But she esteams them all

When winters past and snows are gone
The daisys on the road
Tells every happy hastener on
That spring is all abroad

Violets of many sorts are know[n]
But the sweetest yet that grows
Is that which every hedgrow owns
And every body knows

This moss upon the sallow roots
Of this secluded spot
Finds seasons that its [temper] suits
And blossoms unforgot

Why need I sigh for hills to see
If grass be their array
While here the little paths go through
The grasses every day

Such fancy fills the restless mind
At once to cheat and cheer
With thought and zemblance undefined
No where and everywhere

The fields are pleasing every day
Where thought so full of talk
Through autumn brown and winter grey
Meets pleasure in the walk

It peeps among the fallen leaves
On every stoven* grows
Sufficient sun its shade recieves
And so it buds and blows

O natures pleasant moods and dreams
In every journey lies
That glads my heart with simple themes
And cheers and gratifyes

Thus common things in every place
Their pleasing lessons give
They teach my heart lifes good to trace
And learn me how to live

They feed my heart with one consent
That humble hope and fear
That quiet peace and calm content
Are blessings every where

Labours Leisure

O FOR the feelings and the carless health
That found me toiling in the fields—the joy
I felt at eve with not a wish for wealth
When labour done and in the hedge put bye
My delving spade—I homeward used to hie
With thoughts of books I often read by stealth
Beneath the blackthorn clumps at dinners hour
It urged my weary feet with eager speed
To hasten home where winter fires did shower
Scant light now felt as beautiful indeed
Where bending oer my knees I used to read
With earnest heed all books that had the power
To give me joy in most delicious ways
And rest my spirits after weary days

Aye when long summer showers lets labour win
Sweet leisure—how I used to mark with joy
The south grow black and blacker to the eye
Till the rain came and pessed* me to the skin

No matter anxious happiness was bye
With her refreshing pictures through the rain
Carless of bowering bush and sheltering tree
I homeward hied to feed on books again
For they were then a very feast to me
The simplest things were sweetest melody
And nothing met my eager taste in vain
And thus to read I often wished for rain
Such leisure fancys fed my lowly lot
Possessing nothing and still wanting not

It is an happiness that simplest hearts
Find their own joy in what they undertake
That nature like the seasons so imparts
That every mind its own home comfort makes
That be our dwelling in the fields or woods
No matter custom so endears the scenes
We feel in lonliness sweet company
And many a varied pleasure intervenes
Which the wide world unnoting passes bye
Pursuing what delights it varied joy
Thus happiness is with us joys succeed
Spontaneous everywhere like summer weeds
The cheerful commoners of every spot
Blessing the highest and the lowliest lot

The Woodman

Now evening comes and from the new laid hedge
The woodman rustles in his leathern guise
Hiding in dyke ylined with brustling* sedge
His bill and mattock from thefts meddling eyes
And in his wallets storing many a pledge
Of flowers and boughs from early sprouting trees
And painted pootys from the ivied hedge
About its mossy roots his boys to please
Who wait with merry joy his coming home
Anticipating presents such as these

Gained far afield where they nor night nor morn
Find no school leisure long enough to go
Where flowers but rarely from their stalks are torn
And birds scarce loose a nest the season through

✧✧✧

I CAME to the flood washd mead or stream and then my tackle was
eagerly fastend on and my heart woud thrill with hopes of success as
I saw a sizable gudgeon twinkle round the glossy pebbles or a fish
leap after a flye or a floating somthing on the deeper water   were is
the angler that hath not felt these delights in his young days and were
is an angler that doth not feel taken with their memory when he is
old?

✧✧✧

Angling

ANGLING has pleasures that are much enjoyed
By tasteful minds of nature never cloyed
In pleasant solitudes where winding floods
Pass level meadows of oerhanging woods
Verged with tall reeds that rustle in the wind
A soothing music in the anglers mind
A rush right complasant that ever bows
Obesceience to the stream that laughs below
He feels delighted into quiet praise
And sweet the pictures that the mind essays
While gentle whispers on the southern wind
Brings health and quiet to the anglers mind
Smooth as the gentle river whirls along
And sweet as memory of some happy song

The morn is still and balmy all that moves
The trees are south gales which the angler loves
That stirs the waving grass in idle whirls
And flush the cheeks and fan the jetty curls
Of milking maidens at their morns employ
Who sing and wake the dewy fields to joy

The sun just rising large and round and dim
Keeps creeping up oer the flat meadows brim
As rising from the ground to run its race
Till up it mounts and shows a ruddy face
Now is the time the angler leaves his dreams
In anxious movements for the silent streams
Frighting the heron from its morning toil
First at the river watching after spoil

Now with the rivers brink he winds his way
For a choice place to spend the quiet day
Marking its banks how varied things appear
Now cloathed in trees and bushes and now clear
While steep the bank climbs from the waters edge
Then almost choaked with rushes flags and sedge
Then flat and level to the very brink
Tracked deep by cattle running there to drink
At length he finds a spot half shade half sun
That scarcely curves to show the waters run
Still clear and smooth quick he his line unlaps
While fish leap up and loud the water claps
Which fills his mind with pleasures of surprise
That in the deep hole some old monster lies

Right cautious now his strongest line to take
Lest some hugh monster should his tackle break
Then half impatient with a cautious throw
He swings his line into the depths below
The water rat hid in the shivering reeds
That feeds upon the slime and water weeds
Nibbling their grassy leaves with crizzling* sound
Plunges below and makes his fancys bound
With expectations joy—down goes the book
In which glad leisure might for pleasure look
And up he grasps the angle in his hand
In readiness the expected prize to land
While tip toe hope gives expectations dream
Bright as the sunshine sleeping on the stream

None but true anglers feel that gush of joy
That flushes in the patient minds employ
While expectation upon tip toe sees
The float just wave it cannot be a breeze
For not a waver oer the waters pass
Warm with the joyous day and smooth as glass
Now stronger moved it dances round then stops
Then bobs again and in a moment drops
Beneath the water—he with joys elate
Pulls and his rod bends double with the weight
True was his skill in hopes expecting dream
And up he draws a flat and curving bream
That scarcely landed from the tackle drops
And on the bank half thronged in sedges stops

Now sport the waterflyes with tiny wings
A dancing crowd imprinting little rings
And the rich light the suns young splendours throw
Is by the very pebbles caught below
Behind the leaning tree he stoops to lean
And soon the stirring float again is seen
A larger yet from out its ambush shoots
Hid underneath the old trees cranking* roots
The float now shakes and quickens his delight
Then bobs a moment and is out of sight
Which scarce secured down goes the cork again
And still a finer pants upon the plain
And bounds and flounces mid the new mown hay
And luck but ceases with the closing day

I HAVE often wondered how birds nests escape injuries which are
built upon the ground   I have found larks nests in an old cart rut
grassed over and pettichaps close on the edge of a horse track in a
narrow lane where two carts could not pass and two oxen would even
have difficulty in doing so but yet I never found a nest destroyed
providence was their protector   and on the cow pasture I have often
seen an hungry ox sturt its head on one side making a snufting

noise and cease eating for a minute or two and then turn in another direction and on going to see what it turned from I have started up the old bird and found its nest often by this sign

The nightingales nest in the orchard hedge was composed without side of dead maple leaves and some oak leaves and lined within with withered grass and a few fragments of oak leaves

Long tailed titmouse and Chaffinch and red cap make a most beautiful outside to their nests of grey lichen   linnets and hedgsparrows make a loose ruff outside of coarse green moss wool and roots   the first are like the freestone fabrics of finished ellegance   the latter like the rough plain walls of a husbandman's cottage yet equally warm and comfortable within   Pinks* use cowhair and some feathers for their inside hangings   redcaps get thistle down   hedge sparrows use wool and cowhair intermixed   linnets use wool and cowhair and the furze linnet uses rabbit down   these four sorts of birds never (I think) are known to use horse hair while yellow hammers ground larks yellow wagtails and skylarks never use wool or cowhair but on the contrary small roots and horse hair and this universaly   bulfinches make a slight nest of sticks and small roots very shallow whitethroats use dead hariff* stalks linked with cobwebs and lined with fine roots and horsehair

The Eternity of Nature

LEAVES from eternity are simple things
To the worlds gaze—whereto a spirit clings
Sublime and lasting—trampled under foot
The daisy lives and strikes its little root
Into the lap of time—centurys may come
And pass away into the silent tomb
And still the child hid in the womb of time
Shall smile and pluck them when this simple ryhme
Shall be forgotten like a churchyard stone
Or lingering lie unnoticed and alone

When eighteen hundred years our common date
Grows many thousands in their marching state
Aye still the child with pleasure in its eye
Shall cry the daisy—a familiar cry
And run to pluck it—in the self same state
As when time found it in his infant date
And like a child himself when all was new
Wonder might smile and make him notice too
—Its little golden bosom frilled with snow
Might win een Eve to stoop adown and show
Her partner Adam in the silky grass
This little gem that smiled where pleasure was
And loving Eve from eden followed ill
And bloomed with sorrow and lives smiling still
As once in eden under heavens breath
So now on blighted earth and on the lap of death
It smiles for ever—cows laps golden blooms
That in the closen and the meadow comes
Shall come when kings and empires fade and die
And in the meadows as times partners lie
As fresh two thousand years to come as now
With those five crimson spots upon its brow
And little brooks that hum a simple lay
In green unnoticed spots from praise away
Shall sing when poets in times darkness hid
Shall lie like memory in a pyramid
Forgetting yet not all forgot—tho lost
Like a threads end in ravelled windings crost
And the small bumble bee shall hum as long
As nightingales for time protects the song
And nature is their soul to whom all clings
Of fair or beautiful in lasting things
The little robin in the quiet glen
Hidden from fame and all the strife of men
Sings unto time a pastoral and gives
A music that lives now and ever lives
Both spring and autumn years rich bloom and fade
Longer then songs that poets ever made
And think ye these times play things—pass proud skill

Time loves them like a child and ever will
And so I worship them in bushy spots
And sing with them when all else notice not
And feel the music of their mirth agree
With that sooth quiet that bestirreth me
And if I touch aright that quiet tone
That soothing truth that shadows from their own
Then many a year shall grow in after days
And still find hearts to read my quiet lays
Yet cheering mirth with thoughts sung not for fame
But for the joy that with their utterance came
That inward breath of rapture urged not loud
—Birds singing lone flie silent past the crowd
So in these pastoral spots which childish time
Makes dear to me I sit me down and ryhme
What time the dewy mornings infancy
Hangs on each blade of grass and every tree
And sprents the red thighs of the bumble bee
Who gins by times unwearied minstrelsy
Who breakfasts dines and most divinely sups
With every flower save golden butter cups
On their proud bosoms he will never go
And passes bye with scarcely how do ye do
So in these showy gaudy shining cells
May be the summers honey never dwells
—Her ways are mysterys all yet endless youth
Lives in them all unchangable as truth
With the odd number five strange natures laws
Plays many freaks nor once mistakes the cause
And in the cowslap peeps this very day
Five spots appear which time neer wears away
Nor once mistakes the counting—look within
Each peep and five nor more nor less is seen
And trailing bindweed with its pinky cup
Five lines of paler hue goes streaking up
And birds a many keep the rule alive
And lay five eggs nor more nor less then five
And flowers how many own that mystic power
With five leaves making up the flower

The five leaved grass trailing its golden cups
Of flowers—five leaves make all for which I stoop
And briony in the hedge that now adorns
The tree to which it clings and now the thorns
Own five star pointed leaves of dingy white
Count which I will all make the number right
And spreading goosegrass trailing all abroad
In leaves of silver green about the road
Five leaves make every blossom all along
I stoop for many none are counted wrong
Tis natures wonder and her makers will
Who bade earth be and order owns him still
As that superior power who keeps the key
Of wisdom power and might through all eternity

Shadows of Taste

TASTE with as many hues doth hearts engage
As leaves and flowers do upon natures page
Not mind alone the instinctive mood declares
But birds and flowers and insects are its heirs
Taste is their joyous heritage and they
All choose for joy in a peculiar way
Birds own it in the various spots they chuse
Some live content in low grass gemmed with dews
The yellow hammer like a tasteful guest
Neath picturesque green molehills makes a nest
Where oft the shepherd with unlearned ken
Finds strange eggs scribbled as with ink and pen
He looks with wonder on the learned marks
And calls them in his memory writing larks
Birds bolder winged on bushes love to be
While some choose cradles on the highest tree
There rocked by winds they feel no moods of fear
But joy their birthright lives for ever near
And the bold eagle which mans fear enshrouds
Would could he lodge it house upon the clouds
While little wrens mistrusting none that come

In each low hovel meet a sheltered home
Flowers in the wisdom of creative choice
Seem blest with feeling and a silent voice
Some on the barren roads delight to bloom
And others haunt the melancholly tomb
Where death the blight of all finds summers hours
Too kind to miss him with her host of flowers
Some flourish in the sun and some the shade
Who almost in his morning smiles would fade
These in leaf darkened woods right timid stray
And in its green night smile their lives away
Others in water live and scarcely seem
To peep their little flowers above the stream
While water lilies in their glories come
And spread green isles of beauty round their home
All share the summers glory and its good
And taste of joy in each peculiar mood
Insects of varied taste in rapture share
The heyday luxuries which she comes to heir
In wild disorder various routs they run
In water earth still shade and busy sun
And in the crowd of green earths busy claims
They een grow nameless mid their many names
And man that noble insect restless man
Whose thoughts scale heaven in its mighty span
Pours forth his living soul in many a shade
And taste runs riot in her every grade
While the low herd mere savages subdued
With nought of feeling or of taste imbued
Pass over sweetest scenes a carless eye
As blank as midnight in its deepest dye
From these and different far in rich degrees
Minds spring as various as the leaves of trees
To follow taste and all her sweets explore
And Edens make where deserts spread before
In poesys spells some all their raptures find
And revel in the melodies of mind
There nature oer the soul her beauty flings
In all the sweets and essences of things

A face of beauty in a city crowd
Met—passed—and vanished like a summer cloud
In poesys vision more refined and fair
Taste reads oerjoyed and greets her image there
Dashes of sunshine and a page of may
Live there a whole life long one summers day
A blossom in its witchery of bloom
There gathered dwells in beauty and perfume
The singing bird the brook that laughs along
There ceasless sing and never thirsts for song
A pleasing image to its page conferred
In living character and breathing word
Becomes a landscape heard and felt and seen
Sunshine and shade one harmonizing green
Where meads and brooks and forrests basking lie
Lasting as truth and the eternal sky
Thus truth to nature as the true sublime
Stands a mount atlas overpeering time
   Styles may with fashions vary—tawdry chaste
Have had their votaries which each fancied taste
From Donns old homely gold whose broken feet
Jostles the readers patience from its seat
To Popes smooth rhymes that regularly play
In musics stated periods all the way
That starts and closes starts again and times
Its tuning gamut true as minster chimes
From these old fashions stranger metres flow
Half prose half verse that stagger as they go
One line starts smooth and then for room perplext
Elbows along and knocks against the next
And half its neighbour where a pause marks time
There the clause ends what follows is for rhyme
Yet truth to nature will in all remain
As grass in winter glorifies the plain
And over fashions foils rise proud and high
As lights bright fountain in a cloudy sky
   The man of science in discoverys moods
Roams oer the furze clad heaths leaf buried woods
And by the simple brook in rapture finds

Treasures that wake the laugh of vulgar hinds
Who see no further in his dark employs
Then village childern seeking after toys
Their clownish hearts and ever heedless eyes
Find nought in nature they as wealth can prize
With them self interest and the thoughts of gain
Are natures beautys all beside are vain
But he the man of science and of taste
Sees wealth far richer in the worthless waste
Where bits of lichen and a sprig of moss
Will all the raptures of his mind engross
And bright winged insects on the flowers of may
Shine pearls too wealthy to be cast away
His joys run riot mid each juicy blade
Of grass where insects revel in the shade
And minds of different moods will oft condemn
His taste as cruel such the deeds to them
While he unconsious gibbets butterflyes
And strangles beetles all to make us wise
Tastes rainbow visions own unnumbered hues
And every shade its sense of taste pursues
The heedless mind may laugh the clown may stare
They own no soul to look for pleasure there
Their grosser feelings in a coarser dress
Mock at the wisdom which they cant possess
Some in recordless rapture love to breath
Natures wild Eden wood and field and heath
In common blades of grass his thoughts will raise
A world of beauty to admire and praise
Untill his heart oerflows with swarms of thought
To that great being who raised life from nought
The common weed adds graces to his mind
And gleams in beautys few beside may find
Associations sweet each object breeds
And fine ideas upon fancy feeds
He loves not flowers because they shed perfumes
Or butterflyes alone for painted plumes
Or birds for singing although sweet it be
But he doth love the wild and meadow lea

There hath the flower its dwelling place and there
The butterflye goes dancing through the air
He loves each desolate neglected spot
That seems in labours hurry left forgot
The crank* and punished trunk of stunted oak
Freed from its bonds but by the thunder stroke
As crampt by struggling ribs of ivy sere
There the glad bird makes home for half the year
But take these several beings from their homes
Each beautious thing a withered thought becomes
Association fades and like a dream
They are but shadows of the things they seem
Torn from their homes and happiness they stand
The poor dull captives of a foreign land
Some spruce and delicate ideas feed
With them disorder is an ugly weed
And wood and heath a wilderness of thorns
Which gardeners shears nor fashions nor adorns
No spots give pleasure so forlorn and bare
But gravel walks would work rich wonders there
With such wild natures beautys run to waste
And arts strong impulse mars the truth of taste
Such are the various moods that taste displays
Surrounding wisdom in concentring rays
Where threads of light from one bright focus run
As days proud halo circles round the sun

The Progress of Ryhme

O SOUL enchanting poesy
Thoust long been all the world with me
When poor thy presence grows my wealth
When sick thy visions gives me health
When sad thy sunny smile is joy
And was from een a tiny boy
When trouble was and toiling care
Seemed almost more then I could bear
While thrashing in the dusty barn

Or squashing in the ditch to earn
A pittance that would scarce alow
One joy to smooth my sweating brow
Where drop by drop would chase and fall
—Thy presence triumphed over all
The vulgar they might frown and sneer
Insult was mean—but never near
Twas poesys self that stopt the sigh
And malice met with no reply
So was it in my earlier day
When sheep to corn had strayed away
Or horses closen gaps had broke
Ere sunrise peeped or I awoke
My masters frown might force the tear
But poesy came to check and cheer
It glistened in my shamed eye
But ere it fell the swoof* was bye
I thought of luck in future days
When even he might find a praise
I looked on poesy like a friend
To cheer me till my life should end
Twas like a parents first regard
And love when beautys voice was heard
Twas joy twas hope and may be fear
But still twas rapture every where
My heart were ice unmoved to dwell
Nor care for one I loved so well
Through rough and smooth through good and ill
That led me and attends me still
It was an early joy to me
That joy was love and poesy
And but for thee my idle lay
Had neer been urged in early day
The harp imagination strung
Had neer been dreamed of—but among
The flowers in summers fields of joy
Id lain an idle rustic boy
No hope to think of fear or care
And even love a stranger there

But poesy that vision flung
Around me as I hummed or sung
I glowered on beauty passing bye
Yet hardly turned my sheepish eye
I worshiped yet could hardly dare
To show I knew the goddess there
Lest my presumptious stare should gain
But frowns ill humour or disdain
My first ambition was its praise
My struggles aye in early days
Had I by vulgar boldness torn
That hope when it was newly born
By rudeness gibes and vulgar tongue
The curse of the unfeeling throng
Their scorn had frowned upon the lay
And hope and song had passed away
And I with nothing to attone
Had felt myself indeed alone
But promises of days to come
The very fields would seem to hum
Those burning days when I should dare
To sing aloud my worship there
When beautys self might turn its eye
Of praise—what could I do but try
Twas winter then—but summer shone
From heaven when I was all alone
And summer came and every weed
Of great or little had its meed
Without its leaves there wa'nt a bower
Nor one poor weed without its flower
Twas love and pleasure all along
I felt that Id a right to song
And sung but in a timid strain
Of fondness for my native plain
For every thing I felt a love
The weeds below the birds above
And weeds that bloomed in summers hours
I thought they should be reckoned flowers
They made a garden free for all

And so I loved them great and small
And sung of some that pleased my eye
Nor could I pass the thistle bye .
But paused and thought it could not be
A weed in natures poesy
No matter for protecting wall
No matter tho they chance to fall
Where sheep and cows and oxen lie
The kindly rain when theyre a dry
Falls on them with as plenteous showers
As when it waters garden flowers
They look up with a blushing eye
Upon a tender watching sky
And still enjoy the kindling smile
Of sunshine tho they live with toil
As garden flowers with all their care
For natures love is even there
And so it cheered me while I lay
Among their beautiful array
To think that I in humble dress
Might have a right to happiness
And sing as well as greater men
And then I strung the lyre agen
And heartened up oer toil and fear
And lived with rapture every where
Till dayshine to my themes did come
Just as a blossom bursts to bloom
And finds its self in thorny ways
So did my musings meet wi praise
And tho no garden care had I
My heart had love for poesy
A simple love a wild esteem
As heart felt as the linnets dream
That mutters in its sleep at night
Some notes from extacys delight
Thus did I dream oer joys and lye
Muttering dream songs of poesy
The night dislimned and waking day
Shook from wood leaves the drops away

Hope came—storms calmed—and hue and cry
With her false pictures herded bye
With tales of help where help was not
Of friends who urged to write or blot
Whose taste were such that mine were shame
Had they not helpt it into fame
Poh—let the idle rumour ill
Their vanity is never still
My harp tho simple was my own
When I was in the fields alone
With none to help and none to hear
To bid me either hope or fear
The bird and bee its chords would sound
The air hummed melodys around
I caught with eager ear the strain
And sung the music oer again
Or love or instinct flowing strong
Fields were the essence of the song
And fields and woods are still as mine
Real teachers that are all divine
So if my song be weak or tame
Tis I not they who bear the blame
But hope and cheer thro good and ill
They are my aids to worship still
Still growing on a gentle tide
Nor foes could mar or friends could guide
Like pasture brooks thro sun and shade
Crooked as channels chance hath made
It rambles as it loves to stray
And hope and feeling leads the way
—Aye birds no matter what the tune
Or 'croak' or 'tweet'—twas natures boon
That brought them joy—and music flung
Its spell oer every mattin sung
And een the sparrows chirp to me
Was song in its felicity
When grief hung oer me like a cloud
Till hope seemed even in her shroud
I whispered poesys spells till they

Gleamed round me like a summers day
When tempests oer my labour sung
My soul to its responses rung
And joined the chorus till the storm
Fell all unheeded void of harm
And each old leaning shielding tree
Were princely pallaces to me
Where I would sit me down and chime
My unheard rhapsodies to ryhme
All I beheld of grand—with time
Grew up to beautifuls sublime
The arching groves of ancient lime
That into roofs like churches climb
Grain intertwisting into grain
That stops the sun and stops the rain
And spreads a gloom that never smiles
Like ancient halls and minster aisles
While all without a beautious screen
Of summers luscious leaves is seen
While heard that ever lasting hum
Of bees that haunt them where they bloom
As tho' twas natures very place
Of worship where her mighty race
Of insect life and spirits too
In summer time were wont to go
Both insects and the breath of flowers
To sing their makers mighty powers
Ive thought so as I used to rove
Thro burghley park that darksome grove
Of limes where twilight lingered grey
Like evening in the midst of day
And felt without a single skill
That instinct that would not be still
To think of song sublime beneath
That heaved my bosom like my breath
That burned and chilled and went and came
Without or uttering or a name
Untill the vision waked with time
And left me itching after ryhme

Where little pictures idly tells
Of natures powers and natures spells
I felt and shunned the idle vein
Laid down the pen and toiled again
But spite of all thro good and ill
It was and is my worship still
No matter how the world approved
Twas nature listened—I that loved
No matter how the lyre was strung
From my own heart the music sprung
The cowboy with his oaten straw
Altho he hardly heard or saw
No more of music then he made
Twas sweet—and when I pluckt the blade
Of grass upon the woodland hill
To mock the birds with artless skill
No music in the world beside
Seemed half so sweet—till mine was tried
So my boy-worship poesy
Made een the muses pleased with me
Untill I even danced for joy
A happy and a lonely boy
Each object to my ear and eye
Made paradise of poesy
I heard the blackbird in the dell
Sing sweet—could I but sing as well
I thought—untill the bird in glee
Seemed pleased and paused to answer me
And nightingales O I have stood
Beside the pingle* and the wood
And oer the old oak railing hung
To listen every note they sung
And left boys making taws of clay
To muse and listen half the day
The more I listened and the more
Each note seemed sweeter then before
And aye so different was the strain
Shed scarce repeat the note again
—'Chew-chew Chew-chew'—and higher still

'Cheer-cheer Cheer-cheer'—more loud and shrill
'Cheer-up Cheer-up cheer-up'—and dropt
Low 'Tweet tweet tweet jug jug jug' and stopt
One moment just to drink the sound
Her music made and then a round
Of stranger witching notes was heard
As if it was a stranger bird
'Wew-wew wew-wew chur-chur chur-chur
'Woo-it woo-it'—could this be her
'Tee-rew Tee-rew tee-rew tee-rew
'Chew-rit chew-rit'—and ever new
'Will-will will-will grig-grig grig-grig'
The boy stopt sudden on the brig
To hear the 'tweet tweet tweet' so shill
Then 'jug jug jug'—and all was still
A minute—when a wilder strain
Made boys and woods to pause again
Words were not left to hum the spell
Could they be birds that sung so well
I thought—and may be more then I
That musics self had left the sky
To cheer me with its magic strain
And then I hummed the words again
Till fancy pictured standing bye
My hearts companion poesy
No friends had I to guide or aid
The struggles young ambition made
In silent shame the harp was tried
And raptures guess the tune applied
Yet oer the songs my parents sung
My ear in silent musings hung
Their kindness wishes did regard
They sung and joy was my reward
All else was but a proud decree
The right of bards and nought to me
A title that I dare not claim
And hid it like a private shame
I whispered aye and felt a fear
To speak aloud tho' none was near

I dreaded laughter more then blame
And dare not sing aloud for shame
So all unheeded lone and free
I felt it happiness to be
Unknown obscure and like a tree
In woodland peace and privacy
No not a friend on earth had I
But my own kin and poesy
Nor wealth—and yet I felt indeed
As rich as any body need
To be—for health and hope and joy
Was mine altho a lonely boy
And what I felt—as now I sing
Made friends of all and every thing
Save man the vulgar and the low
The polished twas not mine to know
Who paid me in my after days
And gave me even more then praise
Twas then I found that friends indeed
Were needed when Id less to need
—The pea that independant springs
—When in its blossom trails and clings
To every help that lingers bye
And I when classed with poesy
Who stood unbrunt* the heaviest shower
Felt feeble as that very flower
And helpless all—but beautys smile
Is harvest for the hardest toil
Whose smiles I little thought to win
With ragged coat and downy chin
A clownish silent haynish* boy
Who even felt ashamed of joy
So dirty ragged and so low
With nought to reccomend or show
That I was worthy een a smile
—Had I but felt amid my toil
That I in days to come should be
A little light in minstrelsy
And in the blush of after days

Win beautys smile and beautys praise
My heart with lonely fancy warm
Had even bursted with the charm
And Mary thou whose very name
I loved whose look was even fame
From those delicious eyes of blue
In smiles and rapture ever new
Thy timid step thy fairy form
Thy face with blushes ever warm
When praise my schoolboy heart did move
I saw thy blush and thought it love
And all ambitious thee to please
My heart was ever ill at ease
I saw thy beauty grow with days
And tryed song-pictures in thy praise
And all of fair or beautiful
Were thine akin—nor could I pull
The blossoms that I thought divine
Lest I should injure aught of thine
So where they grew I let them be
And tho' I dare not look to thee
Of love—to them I talked aloud
And grew ambitious from the crowd
With hopes that I should one day be
Beloved Mary een by thee
But I mistook in early day
The world—and so our hopes decay
Yet that same cheer in after toils
Was poesy—and still she smiles
As sweet as blossoms to the tree
And hope love joy are poesy

ᨆᨆᨆ

March 25th 1825

I TOOK a walk to day to botanize and found that the spring had
taken up her dwelling in good earnest   she has covered the woods
with the white anemonie which the children call Ladysmocks and the
hare bells are just venturing to unfold their blue dropping bells
the green is covered with daiseys and the little Celadine   the hedge

125

bottoms are crowded with the green leaves of the arum were the boy is peeping for pootys with eager anticipations and delight   the sallows are cloathed in their golden palms were the bees are singing a busy welcome to spring   they seem uncommonly fond of these flowers and gather round them in swarms   I have often wondered how these little travellers found their homes agen from the woods and solitudes were they journey for wax and honey   I have seen them to day at least 3 miles from any village in Langley wood working at their palms and some of them with their little thighs so loaded with the yellow dust as to seem almost unable to flye   it is curious to see how they collect their load   they keep wiping their legs over their faces to gather the dust that settles there after creeping in the flowers till they have got a sufficient load and then they flye homward to their hives I have heard that a man curious to know how far his bees travelld in a summers day got up early one morning and stood by one of the hives to powder them as they came out with fine flour to know them agen . . . and having to go to the market that day he passd by a turnip field in full flower about 5 miles from home and to his supprise he found some of his own in their white powderd coats busily huming at their labour with the rest   the Ivy berrys are quite ripe and the wood pigeons are busily fluskering* among the Ivied dotterels* on the skirts of the common . . . have you never heard that cronking* jaring noise in the woods at this early season?   I heard it to day and went into the woods to examine what thing it was that caused the sound and I discoverd that it was the common green woodpecker busily employd at boreing his hole which he effected by twisting his bill round in the way that a carpenter twists his wimble* with this difference that when he has got it to a certain extent he turns it back and then pecks awhile and then twists agen   his beak seems to serve all the purposes of a nail passer* gough* and wimble effectually

ๆๆๆๆ

First sight of Spring

THE hazel blooms in threads of crimson hue
Peep through the swelling buds and look for spring
Ere yet a white thorn leaf appears in view
Or march finds throstles* pleased enough to sing

126

On the old touchwood tree wood peckers cling
A moment and their harsh toned notes renew
In happier mood the stockdove claps his wing
The squirrel sputters* up the powdered oak
With tail cocked oer his head and ears errect
Startled to hear the woodmans understroke
And with the courage that his fears collect
He hisses fierce half malice and half glee
Leaping from branch to branch about the tree
In winters foliage moss and lichens drest

Wood Pictures in Spring

THE rich brown umber hue the oaks unfold
When springs young sunshine bathes their trunks in gold
So rich so beautiful so past the power
Of words to paint—my heart aches for the dower
The pencil gives to soften and infuse
This brown luxuriance of unfolding hues
This living lusious tinting woodlands give
Into a landscape that might breath and live
And this old gate that claps against the tree
The entrance of springs paradise should be
Yet paint itself with living nature fails
—The sunshine threading through these broken rails
In mellow shades—no pencil eer conveys
And mind alone feels fancies and pourtrays

May

THE sunshine bathes in clouds of many hues
And mornings feet are gemmed with early dews
Warm Daffodils about the garden beds
Peep thro their pale slim leaves their golden heads
Sweet earthly suns of spring—the gosling broods
In coats of sunny green about the road
Waddle in extacy—and in rich moods

The old hen leads her flickering chicks abroad
Oft scuttling neath her wings so see the kite
Hang wavering oer them in the springs blue light
The sparrows round their new nests chirp with glee
And sweet the Robin springs young luxury shares
Tuteling its song in feathery gooseberry tree
While watching worms the gardeners spade unbares

Poesy a Maying

Now comes the bonny may dancing and skipping
Accross the stepping stones of meadow streams
Bearing no kin to april showe[r]s a weeping
But constant sunshine as her servant seems
Her heart is up—her sweetness all amaying
Streams in her face like gems on beautys breast
The swains are sighing all and well a daying
Love sick and gazing on their lovely guest
The sunday paths to pleasant places leading
Are graced by couples linking arm in arm
Sweet smiles enjoying or some book areading
Where love and beauty are the constant charm
For while the bonny may is dancing bye
Beauty delights the ear and beauty fills the eye

The birds they sing and build and nature scorns
On mays young festival to keep a widow
There childern too have pleasures all their own
A plucking lady smocks along the meadow
The little brook sings loud among the pebbles
So very loud that water flowers which lie
Where many a silver curdle boils and dribbles
Dance too with joy as it goes singing bye
Among the pasture molehills maidens stoop
To pluck the luscious majoram* for their bosoms
The greenswards smothered oer with buttercups
And white thorns they are breaking down with blossoms
Tis natures livery for the bonny may
Who keeps her court and all have holiday

Princess of months—so natures choice ordains
And lady of the summer still she reigns
In spite of aprils youth who charms in tears
And rosey june who wins with blushing face
July sweet shepherdess who wreaths the shears
Of shepherds with her flowers of winning grace
And sun tanned august with her swarthy charms
The beautiful and rich—and pastoral gay
September with her pomp of fields and farms
And wild novembers sybilline array
In spite of beautys calender the year
Garlands with beautys prize the bonny may
Where ere she goes fair nature hath no peer
And months do loose their queen when shes away

Up like a princess starts the merry morning
In draperies of many coloured cloud
And sky larks minstrels of the early dawning
Pipe forth their hearty anthems long and loud
The bright enarmoured* sunshine goes a maying
And every flower his laughing eye beguiles
And on the milkmaids rosey face a playing
Pays court to beauty in its softest smiles
For mays divinity of joy begun
Adds life and lustre to the golden sun
And all of life beneath its glory straying
Is by mays beauty into worship won
Till golden eve ennobles all the west
And day goes blushing like a bride to rest

Wood pictures in Summer

THE one delicious green that now prevades*
The woods and fields in endless lights and shades
And that deep softness of delicious hues
That overhead blends—softens—and subdues
The eye to extacy and fills the mind
With views and visions of enchanting kind

129

While on the velvet down beneath the swail*
I sit on mossy stulp and broken rail
Or lean oer crippled gate by hugh old tree
Broken by boys disporting there at swee*
While sunshine spread from an exaustless sky
Gives all things extacy as well as I
And all wood-swaily places even they
Are joys own tennants keeping holiday

The Summer Shower

I LOVE it well oercanopied in leaves
Of crowding woods to spend a quiet hour
And where the woodbine weaves
To list the summer shower

Brought by the south west wind that balm and bland
Breaths luscious coolness loved and felt by all
While on the uplifted hand
The rain drops gently fall

Now quickening on and on the pattering woods
Recieves the coming shower birds trim their wings
And in a joyful mood
The little wood chat sings

And blackbird squatting in her mortared nest
Safe hid in ivy and the pathless wood
Pruneth her sooty breast
And warms her downy brood

And little Pettichap like hurrying mouse
Keeps nimbling near my arbour round and round
Aye theres her oven house*
Built nearly on the ground

Of woodbents withered straws and moss and leaves
And lined with downy feathers safteys joy
Dwells with the home she weaves
Nor fears the pilfering boy

The busy falling rain increases now
And sopping leaves their dripping moisture pour
And from each loaded bough
Fast falls the double shower

Weed climbing hedges banks and meeds unmown
Where rushy fringed brooklet easy curls
Look joyous while the rain
Strings their green suit [with] pearls

While from the crouching corn the weeding troop
Run hastily and huddling in a ring
Where the old willows stoop
Their ancient ballads sing

And gabble over wonders ceaseless tale
Till from the south west sky showers thicker come
Humming along the vale
And bids them hasten home

With laughing skip they stride the hasty brook
That mutters through the weeds untill it gains
A clear and quiet nook
To greet the dimpling rain

And on they drabble* all in mirth not mute
Leaving their footmarks on the elting* soil
Where print of sprawling foot
Stirs up a tittering smile

On beautys lips who slipping mid the crowd
Blushes to have her anckle seen so high
Yet inly feeleth proud
That none a fault can spy

Yet rudely followed by the meddling clown
Who passes vulgar gibes—the bashful maid
Lets go her folded gown
And pauses half afraid

131

To climb the stile before him till the dame
To quarrel half provoked assails the knave
And laughs him into shame
And makes him well behave

Bird nesting boys oertaken in the rain
Beneath the ivied maple bustling run
And wait in anxious pain
Impatient for the sun

And sigh for home yet at the pasture gate
The molehill tossing bull with straining eye
Seemeth their steps to wait
Nor dare they pass him bye

Till wearied out high over hedge they scrawl*
To shun the road and through the wet grass roam
Till wet and draggled all
They fear to venture home

The plough team wet and dripping plashes home
And on the horse the ploughboy lolls along
Yet from the wet grounds come
The loud and merry song

Now neath the leafy arch of dripping bough
That loaded trees form oer the narrow lane
The horse released from plough
Naps the moist grass again

Around their blanket camps the gipseys still
Heedless of showers while black thorns shelter round
Jump oer the pasture hills
In many an idle bound

From dark green clumps among the dripping grain
The lark with sudden impulse starts and sings
And mid the smoaking rain
Quivers her russet wings

A joy inspiring calmness all around
Breaths a refreshing sense of strengthening power
Like that which toil hath found
In sundays leisure hour

When spirits all relaxed heart sick of toil
Seeks out the pleasant woods and shadowy dells
And where the fountain boils
Lye listening distant bells

Amid the yellow furze the rabbits bed
Labour hath hid his tools and oer the heath
Hies to the milking shed
That stands the oak beneath

And there he wiles the pleasant shower away
Filling his mind with store of happy things
Rich crops of corn and hay
And all that plenty brings

The crampt horison now leans on the ground
Quiet and cool and labours hard employ
Ceases while all around
Falls a refreshing joy

The Wheat ripening

WHAT time the wheat field tinges rusty brown
And barley bleaches in its mellow grey
Tis sweet some smooth mown baulk to wander down
Or cross the fields on footpaths narrow way
Just in the mealy light of waking day
As glittering dewdrops moist the maidens gown
And sparkling bounces from her nimble feet
Journeying to milking from the neighbouring town
Making life bright with song—and it is sweet
To mark the grazing herds and list the clown

Urge on his ploughing team with cheering calls
And merry shepherds whistling toils begun
And hoarse tongued bird boy whose unceasing calls
Join the larks ditty to the rising sun

Autumn

SYREN of sullen moods and fading hues
Yet haply not incapable of joy
    Sweet autumn I thee hail
    With welcome all unfeigned
And oft as morning from her lattice peeps
To beckon up the sun I seek with thee
    To drink the dewy breath
    Of fields left fragrant then

To solitudes where no frequented paths
But what thine own feet makes betray thy home
    Stealing obtrusive there
    To meditate thine end
By overshadowed ponds in woody nooks
With ramping* sallows lined and crowding sedge
    Who woo the winds to play
    And with them dance for joy

And meadow pools torn wide by lawless floods
Where water lilies spread their oily leaves
    On which as wont the flye
    Oft battens in the sun
Where leans the mossy willow half way oer
On which the shepherd crawls astride to throw
    His angle clear of weeds
    That crowd the waters brim

Or crispy hills and hollows scant of sward
Where step by step the patient lonely boy
    Hath cut rude flights of stairs
    To climb their steepy sides

Then tracking at their feet grown hoarse with noise
The crawling brook that ekes its weary speed
    And struggles thro the weeds
    With faint and sullen brawls

These haunts long favoured but the more as now
With thee thus wandering moralizing on
    Stealing glad thoughts from grief
    And happy tho I sigh
Sweet vision with the wild dishevelled hair
And raiments shadowy of each winds embrace
    Fain would I win thine harp
    To one accordant theme

Now not inaptly craved communing thus
Beneath the curdled* arms of this stunt* oak
    We'll pillow on the grass
    Our thoughts and ruminate
Oer the disorderd scenes of woods and fields
Ploughed lands thin travelled with half hungry sheep
    Pastures tracked deep with cows
    And small birds seeking seeds

Marking the cowboy that so merry trills
His frequent unpremeditated song
    Wooing the winds to pause
    Till echo brawls again
As on with plashy step and clouted* shoon
He roves half indolent and self employed
    To rob the little birds
    Of hips and pendant awes

And sloes dim covered as with dewy veils
And rambling bramble berries pulp and sweet
    Arching their prickly trails
    Half oer the narrow lane
And mark the hedger front with stubborn face
The dank blea wind that whistles thinly bye
    His leathern garb thorn proof
    And cheeks red hot with toil

[While o'er the pleachy lands of mellow brown
The mower's stubbling scythe clogs to his foot
    The ever eking whisp
    With sharp and sudden jerk,
Till into formal rows the russet shocks
Crowd the blank field to thatch time-weathered barns,
    And hovels rude repair,
    Stript by disturbing winds.

See! from the rustling scythe the haunted hare
Scampers circuitous, with startled ears
    Prickt up, then squat, as by
    She brushes to the woods,
Where reeded grass, breast-high and undisturbed,
Forms pleasant clumps, through which the soothing winds
    Soften her rigid fears,
    And lull to calm repose.][1]

Wild sorceress me thy restless mood delights
More than the stir of summers crowded scenes
    Where jostled in the din
    Joy pauled mine ear with song
Heart sickening for the silence that is thine
Not broken inharmoniously as now
    That lone and vagrant bee
    Booms faint its weary chime

And filtering winds thin winnowing thro the woods
In tremelous noise that bids at every breath
    Some sickly cankered leaf
    Let go its hold and die
And now the bickering storm with sudden start
In flirting fits of anger carpeth loud
    Thee urging to thine end
    Sore wept by troubled skyes

And yet sublime in grief thy thoughts delight
To show me visions of most gorgeous dyes
    Haply forgetting now
    They but prepare thy shroud

    [1] Taken from Clare, *The Rural Muse*, 1835.

Thy pencil dashing its excess of shades
Improvident of waste till every bough
    Burns with thy mellow touch
    Disorderly divine

Soon must I mark thee like a pleasant dream
Droop faintly and so sicken for thine end
    As sad the winds sink low
    In dirges for their queen
While in the moment of their weary pause
To cheer thy bankrupt pomp the willing lark
    Starts from its shielding clod
    Sweet snatching scraps of song

Thy life is waining now and silence tries
To mourn but meets no sympathy in sounds
    As stooping low she bends
    Forming with leaves thy grave
To sleep inglorious there mid tangled woods
Till parch lipped summer pines in drought away
    Then from thine ivied trance
    Awake to glories new

Nutters

THE rural occupations of the year
Are each a fitting theme for pastoral song
And pleasing in our autumn paths appear
The groups of nutters as they chat along
The woodland rides in strangest dissabille
Maids jacketed grotesque in garments ill
Hiding their elegance of shape—her ways
Her voice of music makes her woman still
Aught else the error of a carless gaze
Might fancy uncouth rustics noising bye
With laugh and chat and scraps of morning news
Till met the hazel shades and in they hie
Garbed suiting to the toil—the morning dews
Among the underwood are hardly dry

Yet down with crack and rustle branches come
And springing up like bow unloosed when free
Of their ripe clustering bunches brown—while some
Are split and broken under many a tree
Up springs the blundering pheasant with the noise
Loud brawls the maiden to her friends scared sore
And loud with mimic voice mischevous boys
Ape stranger voices to affright her more
Eccho long silent answers many a call
Straggling about the wildwoods guessing way
Till by the woodside waiting one and all
They gather homward at the close of day
While maids with hastier step from sheperds brawl
Speed on half shamed of their strange dissaray

Nutting

THE sun had stooped his westward clouds to win
Like weary traveller seeking for an Inn
When from the hazelly wood we glad descried
The ivied gateway by the pasture side
Long had we sought for nutts amid the shade
Where silence fled the rustle that we made
When torn by briars and brushed by sedges rank
We left the wood and on the velvet bank
Of short sward pasture ground we sat us down
To shell our nutts before we reached the town
The near hand stubble field with mellow glower
Showed the dimmed blaze of poppys still in flower
And sweet the molehills smelt we sat upon
And now the thymes in bloom but where is pleasure gone

Emmonsails Heath in winter

I LOVE to see the old heaths withered brake
Mingle its crimpled* leaves with furze and ling
While the old heron from the lonely lake
Starts slow and flaps his melancholly wing

And oddling* crow in idle motion swing
On the half rotten ash trees topmost twig
Beside whose trunk the gipsey makes his bed
Up flies the bouncing woodcock from the brig*
Where a black quagmire quakes beneath the tread
The field fare chatter in the whistling thorn
And for the awe* round fields and closen* rove
And coy bumbarrels* twenty in a drove
Flit down the hedge rows in the frozen plain
And hang on little twigs and start again

Winter Fields

O FOR a pleasant book to cheat the sway
Of winter—where rich mirth with hearty laugh
Listens and rubs his legs on corner seat
For fields are mire and sludge—and badly off
Are those who on their pudgy* paths delay
There striding shepherd seeking driest way
Fearing nights wetshod feet and hacking cough
That keeps him waken till the peep of day
Goes shouldering onward and with ready hook
Progs* oft to ford the sloughs that nearly meet
Accross the lands—croodling* and thin to view
His loath dog follows—stops and quakes and looks
For better roads—till whistled to pursue
Then on with frequent jump he hirkles* through

Christmass

CHRISTMASS is come and every hearth
Makes room to give him welcome now
Een want will dry its tears in mirth
And crown him wi a holly bough
Tho tramping neath a winters sky
Oer snow track paths and ryhmey stiles
The huswife sets her spining bye
And bids him welcome wi her smiles

The shepherd now no more afraid
Since custom doth the chance bestow
Starts up to kiss the giggling maid
Beneath the branch of mizzletoe
That neath each cottage beam is seen
Wi pearl-like-berrys shining gay
The shadow still of what hath been
Which fashion yearly fades away

And singers too a merry throng
At early morn wi simple skill
Yet imitate the angels song
And chant their christmass ditty still
And mid the storm that dies and swells
By fits—in humings softly steals
The music of the village bells
Ringing round their merry peals

And when its past a merry crew
Bedeckt in masks and ribbons gay
The 'Morrice danse' their sports renew
And act their winter evening play
The clown-turnd-kings for penny praise
Storm wi the actors strut and swell
And harlequin a laugh to raise
Wears his hump back and tinkling bell

And oft for pence and spicy ale
Wi winter nosgays pind before
The wassail singer tells her tale
And drawls her christmass carrols oer
The prentice boy wi ruddy face
And ryhme bepowderd dancing locks
From door to door wi happy pace
Runs round to claim his 'christmass box'

AND then the year usd to be crownd with its holidays as thick as the boughs on a harvest home   there was the long wishd for Christmass day the celebrated week with two sundays when we usd to watch the clerk return with his bundle of ever greens and run for our bunch to stick* the windows and empty candlesticks hanging in the corner or hasten to the woods to gett ivy branches with its joccolate berrys which our parents usd to color with whitening and the bluebag sticking the branches behind the pictures on the walls

⌇⌇⌇⌇⌇

Winter

OLD January clad in crispy rime
Comes hirpling* on and often makes a stand
The hasty snowstorm neer disturbs his time
He mends no pace but beats his dithering hand
And February like a timid maid
Smiling and sorrowing follows in his train
Huddled in cloak of mirey roads affraid
She hastens on to greet her home again
Then March the prophetess by storms inspired
Gazes in rapture on the troubled sky
And then in headlong fury madly fired
She bids the hail storm boil and hurry bye
Yet neath the blackest cloud a sunbeam flings
Its cheering promise of returning spring

Wood pictures in winter

THE woodland swamps with mosses varified
And bullrush forrests bowing by the side
Of shagroot sallows that snug shelter make
For the coy morehen in her bushy lake
Into whose tide a little runnel weaves
Such charms for silence through the choaking leaves

A whimpling* melodys that but intrude
As lullabys to ancient solitude
The wood grass plats which last year left behind
Weaving their feathery lightness to the wind
Look now as picturesque amid the scene
As when the summer glossed their stems in green
While hasty hare brunts* through the creepy gap
Seeks the soft beds and squats in safetys lap

BLACKBIRDS and Thrushes particularly the former feed in hard
winters upon the shell snail horns by hunting them from the hedge
bottoms and wood stulps and taking them to a stone where they brake
them in a very dexterous manner   any curious observer of nature
may see in hard frosts the shells of pootys thickly litterd round a
stone in the lanes and if he waits a short time he will quickly see one
of these birds coming with a snailhorn in his bill which he constantly
taps on the stone till it is broken   he then extracts the snail and like
a true sportsman eagerly hastens to hunt them again in the hedges
or woods where a frequent rustle of their little feet is heard among
the dead leaves

Signs of Winter

TIS winter plain the images around
Protentious* tell us of the closing year
Short grows the stupid day the moping fowl
Go roost at noon—upon the mossy barn
The thatcher hangs and lays the frequent yaum*
Nudged close to stop the rain that drizzling falls
With scarce one interval of sunny sky
For weeks still leeking on that sulky gloom
Muggy and close a doubt twixt night and day
The sparrow rarely chirps the thresher pale

Twanks* with sharp measured raps the weary frail*
Thump after thump right tiresome to the ear
The hedger lonesome brustles at his toil
And shepherds trudge the fields without a song

The cat runs races with her tail—the dog
Leaps oer the orchard hedge and knarls* the grass
The swine run round and grunt and play with straw
Snatching out hasty mouthfuls from the stack
Sudden upon the elm tree tops the crows
Unceremonious visit pays and croaks
Then swops* away—from mossy barn the owl
Bobs hasty out—wheels round and scared as soon
As hastily retires—the ducks grow wild
And from the muddy pond fly up and wheel
A circle round the village and soon tired
Plunge in the pond again—the maids in haste
Snatch from the orchard hedge the mizled* cloaths
And laughing hurry in to keep them dry

Snow Storm

WHAT a night the wind howls hisses and but stops
To howl more loud while the snow volly keeps
Insessant batter at the window pane
Making our comfort feel as sweet again
And in the morning when the tempest drops
At every cottage door mountainious heaps
Of snow lies drifted that all entrance stops
Untill the beesom and the shovel gains
The path—and leaves a wall on either side—
The shepherd rambling valleys white and wide
With new sensations his old memorys fills
When hedges left at night no more descried
Are turned to one white sweep of curving hills
And trees turned bushes half their bodys hide

The boy that goes to fodder with supprise
Walks oer the gate he opened yesternight

The hedges all have vanished from his eyes
Een some tree tops the sheep could reach to bite
The novel scene emboldens new delight
And though with cautious steps his sports begin
He bolder shuffles the hugh hills of snow
Till down he drops and plunges to the chin
And struggles much and oft escape to win
Then turns and laughs but dare not further go
For deep the grass and bushes lie below
Where little birds that soon at eve went in
With heads tucked in their wings now pine for day
And little feel boys oer their heads can stray

The Flood

ON Lolham Brigs in wild and lonely mood
Ive seen the winter floods their gambols play
Through each old arch that trembled while I stood
Bent oer its wall to watch the dashing spray
As their old stations would be washed away
Crash came the ice against the jambs and then
A shudder jarred the arches—yet once more
It breasted raving waves and stood agen
To wait the shock as stubborn as before
—White foam brown crested with the russet soil
As washed from new ploughd lands would dart beneath
Then round and round a thousand eddies boil
On tother side—then pause as if for breath
One minute—and ingulphed—like life in death

Whose wrecky stains dart on the floods away
More swift then shadows in a stormy day
Straws trail and turn and steady—all in vain
The engulphing arches shoot them quickly through
The feather dances flutters and again
Darts through the deepest dangers still afloat
Seeming as faireys whisked it from the view
And danced it oer the waves as pleasures boat

Light hearted as a merry thought in may—
Trays—uptorn bushes—fence demolished rails
Loaded with weeds in sluggish motions stray
Like water monsters lost each winds and trails
Till near the arches—then as in affright
It plunges—reels—and shudders out of sight

Waves trough—rebound—and fury boil again
Like plunging monsters rising underneath
Who at the top curl up a shaggy main
A moment catching at a surer breath
Then plunging headlong down and down—and on
Each following boil the shadow of the last
And other monsters rise when those are gone
Crest their fringed waves—plunge onward and are past
—The chill air comes around me ocean blea*
From bank to bank the waterstrife is spread
Strange birds like snow spots oer the huzzing* sea
Hang where the wild duck hurried past and fled
On roars the flood—all restless to be free
Like trouble wandering to eternity

Summer Images

Now swathy summer by rude health embrowned
Presedence takes of rosey fingered spring
And laughing joy with wild flowers prankt* and crowned
    A wild and giddy thing
With health robust from every care unbound
    Comes on the zephers wing
    And cheers the toiling clown

Happy as holiday enjoying face
Loud tongued and 'merry as a marriage bell'
Thy lightsome step sheds joy in every place
    And where the troubled dwell
Thy witching smiles weans them of half their cares
    And from thy sunny spell
    They greet joy unawares

Then with thy sultry locks all loose and rude
And mantle laced with gems of garish light
Come as of wont—for I would fain intrude
   And in the worlds despite
Share the rude mirth that thine own heart beguiles
   If haply so I might
   Win pleasure from thy smiles

Me not the noise of brawling pleasures cheer
In nightly revels or in city streets
But joys which sooth and not distract mine ear
   That one at leisure meets
In the green woods and meadows summer shorn
   Or fields where bee flye greets
   Ones ear with mellow horn

Where green swathed grass hopper on treble pipe
Singeth and danceth in mad hearted pranks
And bees go courting every flower thats ripe
   On baulks* and sunny banks
And droning dragon flye on rude bassoon
   Striveth to give God thanks
   In no discordant tune

Where speckled thrush by self delight embued
Singeth unto himself for joys amends
And drinks the honey dew of solitude
   Where happiness attends
With inbred joy untill his heart oerflows
   Of which the worlds rude friends
   Nought heeding nothing knows

Where the gay river laughing as it goes
Plashes with easy wave its flaggy sides
And to the calm of heart in calmness shows
   What pleasure there abides
To trace its sedgy banks from trouble free
   Spots solitude provides
   To muse and happy be

Or ruminating neath some pleasant bush
On sweet silk grasses stretch me at mine ease
Where I can pillow on the yielding rush
   And acting as I please
Drop into pleasant dreams or musing lye
   Mark the wind shaken trees
   And cloud betravelled sky

And think me how some barter joy for care
And waste lifes summer health in riot rude
Of nature nor of natures sweets aware
   Where passions vain intrude
These by calm musings softened are and still
   And the hearts better mood
   Feels sick of doing ill

Here I can live and at my leisure seek
Joys far from cold restraints—not fearing pride
Free as the winds that breath upon my cheek
   Rude health so long denied
Where poor integrity can sit at ease
   And list self satisfied
   The song of honey bees

And green lane traverse heedless where it goes
Naught guessing till some sudden turn espies
Rude battered finger post that stooping shows
   Where the snug mystery lies
And then a mossy spire with ivy crown
   Clears up the short supprise
   And shows the peeping town

And see the wild flowers in their summer morn
Of beauty feeding on joys luscious hours
The gay convolvulus wreathing round the thorn
   Agape for honey showers
And slender king cup burnished with the dew
   Of mornings early hours
   Like gold yminted new

And mark by rustic bridge oer shallow stream
Cow tending boy to toil unreconsiled
Absorbed as in some vagrant summer dream
    And now in gestures wild
Starts dancing to his shadow on the wall
    Feeling self gratified
    Nor fearing human thrall

Then thread the sunny valley laced with streams
Or forrests rude and the oershadowed brims
Of simple ponds where idle shepherd dreams
    And streaks* his listless limbs
Or trace* hay scented meadow smooth and long
    Where joys wild impulse swims
    In one continued song

I love at early morn from new mown swath*
To see the startled frog his rout* pursue
And mark while leaping oer the dripping path
    His bright sides scatter dew
And early lark that from its bustle flyes—
    To hail his mattin new
    And watch him to the skyes

And note on hedgerow baulks in moisture sprent*
The jetty snail creep from the mossy thorn
In earnest heed and tremolous intent
    Frail brother of the morn
That from the tiney bents* and misted leaves
    Withdraws his timid horn
    And fearful vision weaves

And swallows heed on smoke tanned chimney top
As wont be first unsealing mornings eye
Ere yet the bee hath gleaned one wayward drop
    Of honey on his thigh
And see him seek morns airy couch to sing
    Untill the golden sky
    Besprents his russet wing

And sawning* boy by tanning corn espy
With clapping noise to startle birds away
And hear him bawl to every passer bye
    To know the hour of day
And see the uncradled breeze refreshed and strong
    With waking blossoms play
    And breath eolian song

I love the south west wind or low or loud
And not the less when sudden drops of rain
Moistens my glowing cheek from ebon cloud
    Threatening soft showers again
That over lands new ploughed and meadow grounds
    Summers sweet breath unchains
    And wakes harmonious sounds

Rich music breaths in summers every sound
And in her harmony of varied greens
Woods meadows hedgrows cornfields all around
    Much beauty intervenes
Filling with harmony the ear and eye
    While oer the mingling scenes
    Far spreads the laughing sky

And wind enarmourd aspin—mark the leaves
Turn up their silver lining to the sun
And list the brustling noise that oft decieves
    And make the sheep boy run
The sound so mimics fast approaching showers
    He thinks the rain begun
    And hastes to sheltering bowers

And mark the evening curdle dank and grey
Changing her watchet* hue for sombre weed
And moping owl to close the lids of day
    On drowsy wing proceed
While chickering* cricket tremolous and long
    Lights farewell inly heeds
    And gives it parting song

While pranking* bat its flighty circlet makes
And gloworm burnisheth its lamp anew
Oer meadows dew besprent—and beetle wakes
    Enquiries ever new
Teazing each passing ear with murmurs vain
    As wonting to pursue
    His homeward path again

And catch the melody of distant bells
That on the wind with pleasing hum rebounds
By fitful starts—then musically swells
    Oer the dim stilly grounds
While on the meadow bridge the pausing boy
    Listens the mellow sounds
    And hums in vacant joy

And now the homebound hedger bundles round
His evening faggot and with every stride
His leathern doublet leaves a rusling sound
    Till silly sheep beside
His path start tremolous and once again
    Look back dissatisfied
    And scan the dewy plain

And greet the soothing calm that smoothly stills
Oer the hearts every sense its opiate dews
In meek eyed moods and ever balmy trills
    That softens and subdues
With gentle quiets bland and sober train
    Which dreamy eve renews
    In many a mellow strain

I love to walk the fields they are to me
A legacy no evil can destroy
They like a spell set every rapture free
    That cheered me when a boy
Play pastime—all times blotting pen conseals
    Come like a new born joy
    To greet me in the fields

For natures objects ever harmonize
With emulous taste that vulgar deed anoys
It loves in quiet moods to sympathise
    And meet vibrating joys
Oer natures pleasant things—nor slighting deems
    Pastimes the muse employs
    As vain obtrusive themes

Summer Moods

I LOVE at eventide to walk alone
Down narrow lanes oerhung with dewy thorn
Where from the long grass underneath the snail
Jet black creeps out and sprouts his timid horn
I love to muse oer meadows newly mown
Where withering grass perfumes the sultry air
Where bees search round with sad and weary drone
In vain for flowers that bloomed but newly there
While in the juicey corn the hidden quail
Cries 'wet my foot' and hid as thoughts unborn
The fairy like and seldom-seen land rail
Utters 'craik craik' like voices underground
Right glad to meet the evenings dewy veil
And see the light fade into glooms around

A Autumn Morning

THE autumn morning waked by many a gun
Throws oer the fields her many coloured light
Wood wildly touched close tanned and stubbles dun
A motley paradise for earths delight
Clouds ripple as the darkness breaks to light
And clover fields are hid with silver mist
One shower of cobwebs oer the surface spread
And threads of silk in strange disorder twist

Round every leaf and blossoms bottly head
Hares in the drowning herbage scarcely steal
But on the battered pathway squats abed
And by the cart rut nips her morning meal
Look where we may the scene is strange and new
And every object wears a changing hue

I THOUGHT I was up sooner then usual and before morning was
on the stir out of doors   but I am pleasantly disapointed by the
whistle of the ploughboy past the window making himself merry
and trying to make the dull weather dance to a very pleasant tune
which I know well and yet cannot recollect the song   but there are
hundreds of these pleasant tunes familiar to the plough and the
splashing team and the little fields of spring that have lain out the
brown rest of winter and green into mirth with the sprouting grain
the songs of the sky lark and the old songs and ballads that ever
accompany field happiness in following the plough—but neither
heard known or noticed by all the world beside

Early Images

COME early morning with thy mealy grey
Moist grass and fitful gales that winnow soft
And frequent—Ill be up with early day
And roam the social way where passing oft
The milking maid who greets the pleasant morn
And shepherd with his hook in folded arm
Rocking along accross the bending corn
And hear the many sounds from distant farm
Of cackling hens and turkeys gobbling loud
And teams just plodding on their way to plough
Down russet tracks that strip the closen green
And hear the mellow low of distant cow
And see the mist up creeping like a cloud
From hollow places in the early scene

And mark the jerking swallow jerk and fling
Its flight oer new mown meadows happily
And cuckoo quivering upon narrow wing
Take sudden flitting from the neighbouring tree
And heron stalking solitary thing
Mount up into high travel far away
And that mild indecision hanging round
Skys holding bland communion with the ground
In gentlest pictures of the infant day
Now picturing rain—while many a pleasing sound
Grows mellower distant in the mealy grey
Of dewy pastures and full many a sight
Seems sweeter in its indistinct array
Than when it glows in mornings stronger light

The morning wind

THERES more then music in this early wind
Awaking like a bird refreshed from sleep
And joy what Adam might in eden find
When he with angels did communion keep
It breaths all balm and insence from the sky
Blessing the husbandman with freshening powers
Joys manna from its wings doth fall and lie
Harvests for early wakers with the flowers
The very grass in joys devotion moves
Cowslaps in adoration and delight
This way and that bow to the breath they love
Of the young winds that with the dew pearls play
Till smoking chimneys sicken the young light
And feelings fairey visions fade away

Winter Evening

THE crib stock fothered*—horses suppered up
And cows in sheds all littered down in straw
The threshers gone the owls are left to whoop
The ducks go waddling with distended craw

Through little hole made in the henroost door
And geese with idle gabble never oer
Bate* careless hog untill he tumbles down
Insult provoking spite to noise the more
While fowl high perched blink with contemptuous frown
On all the noise and bother heard below
Over the stable ridge in crowds the crow
With jackdaws intermixed known by their noise
To the warm woods behind the village go
And whistling home for bed go weary boys

Evening school boys

HARKEN that happy shout—the school house door
Is open thrown and out the younkers* teem
Some run to leap frog on the rushy moor
And others dabble in the shallow stream
Catching young fish and turning pebbles oer
For muscle* clams—Look in that mellow gleam
Where the retiring sun that rests the while
Streams through the broken hedge—How happy seem
Those schoolboy friendships leaning oer the stile
Both reading in one book—anon a dream
Rich with new joys doth their young hearts beguile
And the books pocketed most hastily
Ah happy boys well may ye turn and smile
When joys are yours that never cost a sigh

Mist in the Meadows

THE evening oer the meadow seems to stoop
More distant lessens the diminished spire
Mist in the hollows reaks and curdles up
Like fallen clouds that spread—and things retire
Less seen and less—the shepherd passes near
And little distant most grotesquely shades
As walking without legs—lost to his knees
As through the rawky* creeping smoke he wades

Now half way up the arches dissappear
And small the bits of sky that glimmer through
Then trees loose all but tops—while fields remain
As wont—the indistinctness passes bye
The shepherd all his length is seen again
And further on the village meets the eye

Happiness of evening

THE winter wind with strange and fearful gust
Stirs the dark wood and in the lengthy night
Howls in the chimney top while fears mistrust
Listens the noise by the small glimmering light
Of cottage hearth where warm a circle sits
Of happy dwellers telling morts of tales
Where some long memory wakens up by fits
Laughter and fear and over all prevails
Wonder predominant—they sit and hear
The very hours to minutes and the song
Or story be the subject what it may
Is ever found too short and never long
While the uprising tempest loudly roars
And boldest hearts fear stirring out of doors

Fears ignorance their fancy only harms
Doors safely locked fear only entrance wins
While round the fire in every corner warms
Till nearest hitch away and rub their shins
And now the tempest in its plight begins
The shutters jar the woodbine on the wall
Rustles agen the panes and over all
The noisey storm to troublous fancy dins
And pity stirs the stoutest heart to call
'Who's there' as slow the door latch seemly stirred
But nothing answered so the sounds they heard
Was no benighted traveller—and they fall
To telling pleasant tales to conquor fear
And sing a merry song till bed time creepeth near

Cottage Fears

THE evening gathers from the gloomy woods
And darkling creeps oer silent vale and hill
While the snug village in nights happy moods
Is resting calm and beautifully still
The windows gleam with light the yelping curs
That guards the henroost from the thieving fox
Barks now and then as somthing passing stirs
And distant dogs the noises often mocks
While foxes from the woods send dismal cries
Like somthing in distress the cottager
Hears the dread noise and thinks of danger nigh
And locks up door in haste—nor cares to stir
From the snug safety of his humble shed
Then tells strange tales till time to go to bed

ᴖᴄᴖᴄᴖᴄᴖ

'WILL with a whisp' 'Jinny Whisk' 'Jack with a Lanthorn'—in this november month they are often out in the dark misty nights—on Rotten Moor Dead Moor Eastwell moor Banton Green end Lolham Briggs Rinedyke furlong and many other places in the lordship   I have myself seen them on most of these spots   one dark night I was coming accross the new parks when a sudden light wild and pale appea[r]ed all round me on my left hand for a hundred yards or more accompanied by a crackling noise like that of peas straw burning I stood looking for a minute or so and felt rather alarmed when darkness came round me again and one of the dancing jack a la[n]-thorns was whisking away in the distance which caused the odd luminous light round me   crossing the meadow one dark sunday night I saw when coming over the Nunton bridge a light like a lanthorn standing on the wall of the other bridge   I kept my eyes on it for a while and hastened to come up to it but ere I got half over the meadow it suddenly fell and tumbled into the stream   and when I got on the bridge I looked down it and saw the will o whi[s]p vapour like a light in a bladder whisking along close to the water as if swimming along its surface   but what supprised me was that it was going contrary to the stream

Night Wind

DARKNESS like midnight from the sobbing woods
Clamours with dismal tidings of the rain
Roaring as rivers breaking loose in floods
To spread and foam and deluge all the plain
The cotter* listens at his door again
Half doubting wether it be floods or wind
And through the thickening darkness looks affraid
Thinking of roads that travel has to find
Through nights black depths in dangers garb arrayed
And the loud glabber* round the flaze* soon stops
When hushed to silence by the lifted hand
Of fearing dame who hears the noise in dread
And thinks a deluge comes to drown the land
Nor dares she go to bed untill the tempest drops

Sabbath Bells

IVE often on a sabbath day
Where pastoral quiet dwells
Lay down among the new mown hay
To listen distant bells
That beautifully flung the sound
Upon the quiet wind
While beans in blossom breathed around
A fragrance oer the mind

A fragrance and a joy beside
That never wears away
The very air seems deified
Upon a sabbath day

So beautiful the flitting wrack
Slow pausing from the eye
Earths music seemed to call them back
Calm settled in the sky

And I have listened till I felt
A feeling not in words
A love that rudest moods would melt
When those sweet sounds was heard
A melancholly joy at rest
A pleasurable pain
A love a rapture of the breast
That nothing will explain

A dream of beauty that displays
Imaginary joys
That all the world in all its ways
Finds not to realize
All idly stretched upon the hay
The wind flirt fanning bye
How soft how sweetly swept away
The music of the sky

The ear it lost and caught the sound
Swelled beautifully on
A fitful melody around
Of sweetness heard and gone
I felt such thoughts I yearned to sing
The humming airs delight
That seemed to move the swallows wing
Into a wilder flight

The butterflye in wings of brown
Would find me where I lay
Fluttering and bobbing up and down
And settling on the hay

The waving blossoms seemed to throw
Their fragrance to the sound
While up and down and loud and low
The bells were ringing round

Beans in Blossom

THE south west wind how pleasant in the face
It breathes while sauntering in a musing pace
I roam these new ploughed fields and by the side
Of this old wood where happy birds abide
And the rich blackbird through his golden bill
Litters wild music when the rest are still
Now luscious comes the scent of blossomed beans
That oer the path in rich disorder leans
Mid which the bees in busy songs and toils
Load home luxuriantly their yellow spoils
The herd cows toss the molehills in their play
And often stand the strangers steps at bay
Mid clover blossoms red and tawney white
Strong scented with the summers warm delight

Stepping stones

THE stepping stones that stride the meadow streams
Look picturesque amid springs golden gleams
Where steps the traveller with a wary pace
And boy with laughing leisure in his face
Sits on the midmost stone in very whim
To catch the struttles that beneath him swim
While those accross the hollow lakes are bare
And winter floods no more rave dangers there
But mid the scum left where it roared and fell
The schoolboy hunts to find the pooty shell
Yet there the boisterous geese with golden broods
Hiss fierce and daring in their summer moods
The boys pull off their hats while passing bye
In vain to fright—themselves being forced to flie

Pleasant Places

OLD stonepits with veined ivy overhung
Wild crooked brooks oer which is rudely flung
A rail and plank that bends beneath the tread
Old narrow lanes where trees meet over head
Path stiles on which a steeple we espy
Peeping and stretching in the distant sky
And heaths oerspread with furze blooms sunny shine
Where wonder pauses to exclaim 'divine'
Old ponds dim shadowed with a broken tree
These are the picturesque of taste to me
While painting winds to make compleat the scene
In rich confusion mingles every green
Waving the sketchy pencil in their hands
Shading the living scenes to fairy lands

Stray Walks

HOW pleasant are the fields to roam and think
Whole sabbaths through unnoticed and alone
Beside the little mole hill skirted brink
Of the small brook that skips oer many a stone
Or green woodside where many a squatting oak
Far oer grass screeds their white stained branches hing*
Forming in pleasant close a happy seat
To nestle in while small birds chirp and sing
And the loud blackbird will its mate provoke
More louder yet its chorus to repeat
How pleasant is it thus to think and roam
The many paths scarce knowing which to chuse
All full of pleasant scenes—then wander home
And oer the beautys we have met to muse

Tis sunday and the little paths that wind
Through closen green by hedges and wood sides
And like a brook corn crowded slope divides
Of pleasant fields—their frequent passers find

From early morn to mellow close of day
On different errands climbing many stiles
Oer hung with awthorn tempting haste to stay
And cool some moments of the road away
When hot and high the uncheckt summer smiles
Some journeying to the little hamlet hid
In dark surrounding trees to see their friends
While some sweet leisures aimless road pursue
Wherever fancys musing pleasure wends
To woods or lakes or church thats never out of view

Wood Rides

WHO hath not felt the influence that so calms
The weary mind in summers sultry hours
When wandering thickest woods beneath the arms
Of ancient oaks and brushing nameless flowers
That verge the little ride who hath not made
A minutes waste of time and sat him down
Upon a pleasant swell to gaze awhile
On crowding ferns bluebells and hazel leaves
And showers of lady smocks so called by toil
When boys sprote* gathering sit on stulps and weave
Garlands while barkmen pill the fallen tree
—Then mid the green variety to start
Who hath [not] met that mood from turmoil free
And felt a placid joy refreshed at heart

The Ragwort

RAGWORT thou humble flower with tattered leaves
I love to see thee come and litter gold
What time the summer binds her russet sheaves
Decking rude spots in beautys marigold
That without thee were dreary to behold

Sun burnt and bare—the meadow bank the baulk
That leads a waggonway through mellow fields
Rich with the tints that harvests plenty yields
Browns of all hues—and every where I walk
Thy waste of shining blossoms richly shields
The sun tanned sward in splendid hues that burn
So bright and glaring that the very light
Of the rich sunshine doth to paleness turn
And seems but very shadows in thy sight

⁓⁓⁓

I ALWAYS admire the kindling freshness that the bark of the different sorts of trees and underwood asume in the forest—the 'foul royce' twigs kindling into a vivid color at their tops as red as woodpiegons claws the ash with its grey bark and black swelling buds the Birch with its 'paper rind' and the darker mottled sorts of hazle black alder with the greener hues of sallows willows and the bramble that still wears its leaves with the privet of a purple hue while the straggling wood briar shines in a brighter and more beautiful green odd forward branches in the new laid hedges of white thorn begin to freshen into green before the arum dare peep out of its hood or the primrose and violet shoot up a new leaf thro the warm moss and ivy that shelter their spring dwellings the furze too on the common wear a fairer green and here and there an odd branch is coverd with golden flowers and the ling or heath nestling among the long grass below (coverd with the witherd flowers of last year) is sprouting up into fresh hopes of spring the fairey rings on the pasture are getting deeper dyes and the water weeds with long silver green blades of grass are mantling the stagnant ponds in their summer liverys

[dated Feb. 7, 1825]

⁓⁓⁓

The Hollow Tree

HOW oft a summer shower hath started me
To seek for shelter in a hollow tree
Old hugh ash dotterel wasted to a shell
Whose vigorous head still grew and flourished well

Where ten might sit upon the battered floor
And still look round discovering room for more
And he who chose a hermit life to share
Might have a door and make a cabin there
They seemed so like a house that our desires
Would call them so and make our gipsey fires
And eat field dinners of the juicey peas
Till we were wet and drabbled* to the knees
But in our old tree house rain as it might
Not one drop fell although it rained till night

Salters Tree

HUGH Elm thy rifted trunk all notched and scarred
Like to a warriors destiny—I love
To stretch me often on such shadowed sward
And hear the sighs of summer leaves above
Or on thy buttressed roots to sit and lean
In carless attitude and there reflect
On times and deeds and darings that have been
Old cast aways now swallowed in neglect
While thou art towering in thy strength of heart
Stirring the soul to vain imaginings
In which lifes sordid being hath no part
The wind in that eternal ditty sings
Humming of future things that burns the mind
To leave some fragment of itself behind

The Crab Tree

SPRING comes anew and brings each little pledge
That still as wont my childish heart decieves
I stoop again for violets in the hedge
Among the ivy and old withered leaves
And often mark amid the clumps of sedge

The pooty shells I gathered when a boy
But cares have claimed me many an evil day
And chilled the relish which I had for joy
Yet when crab blossoms blush among the may
As wont in years gone bye I scramble now
Up mid the bramble for my old esteems
Filling my hands with many a blooming bough
Till the heart stirring past as present seems
Save the bright sunshine of those fairy dreams

The Bull on the Pasture

UPON the common in a motley plight
Horses and cows claim equal common right
Who in their freedom learn mischevious ways
And driveth boys who thither nesting strays
And school boys leave their path in vain to find
A nest—when quickly on the threatening wind
The noisey bull lets terror out of doors
To chase intruders from the cowslap moores
And though a thousand blooms where he runs on
He dare not in his terror stoop for one
And when they see the urchins run away
Will toss the ground like savages at play
The schoolboy runs and whines and pants for breath
Like fear heart bursting from the chase of death
And through the hedge he tears for safetys lap
While the bull raves on tother side the gap
He sees a nest but dare not stop to see
If eggs or birds within the dwelling be
—Een skewish* poneys show their teeth and kick
If leisure stirs a hand or bears a stick
And at the pointed finger scream and run
Till mischiefs self the dangers forced to shun
And birds are all that whistle where they come
They bite the bush but never hurt their home
And if a larks nest happen where they stray
Theyll snuft—and sturt—and turn another way

So birds are all that make such neighbours friends
And for such faith snug safety makes amends
There on a dotterel oak from year to year
The magpie builds her dwelling void of fear
Which danger guards around—and daring boys
Are seldom found to mar her quiet joys
For though tis easy clomb and far from high
Here many a year she trains her broods to flye
And there upon the awthorn easy seen
The linnet builds in plumage half as green
Yet safe she lives as in a pathless wood
And lays her eggs and rears her little brood
Till from the nest they flye at ease reclined
On some progecting branches while the wind
Fans by the feathers of each downy breast
As soft as slumbers whispers unto rest
While the hoarse bull lord of the pasture reigns
And lives like terror on the rushy plains
And there as soon as pleasure seeking boys
Hear the hoarse noise they startle from their joys
Drop down the rushes which they pulled to tie
The cowslip bunch and leave the nest to flye
For safer scenes where they at peace can find
Their nests and flowers and leave their fears behind
Reading made easy such life pictures own
That still delight from pleasures they have known
I read such little books at leisures will
And joy though broken feels the picture still
I still look oer the cuts* of boys at play
Among old hugh tree trunks or meadow hay
And read me of birdnesters bursting full
Of terror running from a roaring bull
And feel delight as boys with joy can be
To see him safety-pictured on a tree
Upon whose top his hides—while at its foot
The bulls bent head tears at each stubborn root
And then to read the reading just to see
How safety led the climber from the tree
And how the bull rage-weary went away

And left his prisoner pining after play
Who crept from grain to grain—and ventured down
And ran like lightening to the very town
And told on corner stool his dangers oer
And heard his parents cautions—never more
To hurt young birds or venture in the way
Of firey bulls but stay at home to play
And in my stolen walks on after years
The wild bulls dangers murmured in my ears
And now I feel by safetys side a joy
From memorys fears—delightful as a boy

Emmonsales Heath

IN thy wild garb of other times
I find thee lingering still
Furze oer each lazy summit climbs
At natures easy will

Grasses that never knew a scythe
Waves all the summer long
And wild weed blossoms waken blythe
That ploughshares never wrong

Stern industry with stubborn toil
And wants unsatisfied
Still leaves untouched thy maiden soil
In its unsullied pride

The birds still find their summer shade
To build their nests agen
And the poor hare its rushy glade
To hide from savage men

Nature its family protects
In thy security
And blooms that love what man neglects
Find peaceful homes in thee

The wild rose scents thy summer air
And woodbines weave in bowers
To glad the swain sojourning there
And maidens gathering flowers

Creations steps ones wandering meets
Untouched by those of man
Things seem the same in such retreats
As when the world began

Furze ling and brake all mingling free
And grass forever green
All seem the same old things to be
As they have ever been

The brook oer such neglected ground
Ones weariness to sooth
Still wildly threads its lawless bounds
And chafes the pebble smooth

Crooked and rude as when at first
Its waters learned to stray
And from their mossy fountain burst
It washed itself a way

O who can pass such lovely spots
Without a wish to stray
And leave lifes cares a while forgot
To muse an hour away

Ive often met with places rude
Nor failed their sweet to share
But passed an hour with solitude
And left my blessing there

He that can meet the morning wind
And oer such places roàm
Nor leave a lingering wish behind
To make their peace his home

His heart is dead to quiet hours
No love his mind employs
Poesy with him neer shares its flowers
Nor solitude its joys

O there are spots amid thy bowers
Which nature loves to find
Where spring drops round her earliest flowers
Uncheckt by winters wind

Where cowslips wake the childs supprise
Sweet peeping ere their time
Ere april spreads her dappled skyes
Mid mornings powdered rime

Ive stretched my boyish walks to thee
When maydays paths were dry
When leaves had nearly hid each tree
And grass greened ancle high

And mused the sunny hours away
And thought of little things
That childern mutter oer their play
When fancy trys its wings

Joy nursed me in her happy moods
And all lifes little crowd
That haunt the waters fields and woods
Would sing their joys aloud

I thought how kind that mighty power
Must in his splendour be
Who spread around my boyish hour
Such gleams of harmony

Who did with joyous rapture fill
The low as well as high
And make the pismires round the hill
Seem full as blest as I

Hopes sun is seen of every eye
The haloo that it gives
In natures wide and common sky
Cheers every thing that lives

~~~~

AND be it further Enacted, That no Horses, Beasts, Asses, Sheep,
Lambs, or other Cattle, shall at any Time within the first Ten Years
after the said Allotments shall be directed to be entered upon by the
respective Proprietors thereof, be kept in any of the public Carriage
Roads or Ways to be set out and fenced off on both Sides, or Laned
out in pursuance of this Act.

[From: An Act for Inclosing Lands in the Parishes of Maxey . . .
and Helpstone, in the County of Northampton, 49 Geo. III.
Sess. 1809.]

~~~~

The Mores

FAR spread the moorey ground a level scene
Bespread with rush and one eternal green
That never felt the rage of blundering plough
Though centurys wreathed springs blossoms on its brow
Still meeting plains that stretched them far away
In uncheckt shadows of green brown and grey
Unbounded freedom ruled the wandering scene
Nor fence of ownership crept in between
To hide the prospect of the following eye
Its only bondage was the circling sky
One mighty flat undwarfed by bush and tree
Spread its faint shadow of immensity
And lost itself which seemed to eke its bounds
In the blue mist the orisons edge surrounds

Now this sweet vision of my boyish hours
Free as spring clouds and wild as summer flowers

Is faded all—a hope that blossomed free
And hath been once no more shall ever be
Inclosure came and trampled on the grave
Of labours rights and left the poor a slave
And memorys pride ere want to wealth did bow
Is both the shadow and the substance now
The sheep and cows were free to range as then
Where change might prompt nor felt the bonds of men
Cows went and came with evening morn and night
To the wild pasture as their common right
And sheep unfolded with the rising sun
Heard the swains shout and felt their freedom won
Tracked the red fallow field and heath and plain
Then met the brook and drank and roamed again
The brook that dribbled on as clear as glass
Beneath the roots they hid among the grass
While the glad shepherd traced their tracks along
Free as the lark and happy as her song
But now alls fled and flats of many a dye
That seemed to lengthen with the following eye
Moors loosing from the sight far smooth and blea
Where swopt the plover in its pleasure free
Are vanished now with commons wild and gay
As poets visions of lifes early day
Mulberry bushes where the boy would run
To fill his hands with fruit are grubbed* and done
And hedgrow briars—flower lovers overjoyed
Came and got flower pots—these are all destroyed
And sky bound mores in mangled garbs are left
Like mighty giants of their limbs bereft
Fence now meets fence in owners little bounds
Of field and meadow large as garden grounds
In little parcels little minds to please
With men and flocks imprisoned ill at ease
Each little path that led its pleasant way
As sweet as morning leading night astray
Where little flowers bloomed round a varied host
That travel felt delighted to be lost
Nor grudged the steps that he had taen as vain

When right roads traced his journeys and again
Nay on a broken tree hed sit awhile
To see the mores and fields and meadows smile
Sometimes with cowslaps smothered—then all white
With daiseys—then the summers splendid sight
Of corn fields crimson oer the 'headach' bloomd
Like splendid armys for the battle plumed
He gazed upon them with wild fancys eye
As fallen landscapes from an evening sky
These paths are stopt—the rude philistines thrall
Is laid upon them and destroyed them all
Each little tyrant with his little sign
Shows where man claims earth glows no more divine
But paths to freedom and to childhood dear
A board sticks up to notice 'no road here'
And on the tree with ivy overhung
The hated sign by vulgar taste is hung
As tho the very birds should learn to know
When they go there they must no further go
This with the poor scared freedom bade good bye
And much they feel it in the smothered sigh
And birds and trees and flowers without a name
All sighed when lawless laws enclosure came
And dreams of plunder in such rebel schemes
Have found too truly that they were but dreams

Apology for the Poor

Mr Editor

In this suprising stir of patrioutism and wonderful change in the
ways and opinions of men when your paper is weekly loaded with the
free speech[e]s of county meetings can you find room for mine? or
will you hear the voice of a poor man?—I only wish to ask you a few
plain questions

Amidst all this stir about taxation and tythes and agricultural
distress are the poor to recieve corresponding benefits   they have

been told so I know but it is not the first time they have heard that and been dissapointed   when the tax was taken from leather they was told they should have shoes almost for nothing and they heard the parliment speeches of patriots as the forthcoming propechys of a political millenium but their hopes were soon frost bitten for the tax has long vanished and the price of shoes remains just were it did nay I believe they are a trifle dearer then they was then—thats the only difference   then there was a hue and cry about taking off the duty of Sp[i]ritous liquors and the best Gin was to be little more in price then small beer   the poor man shook his head over such speeches and looking at his shoes had no faith to believe any more of these cheap wonders so he was not dissapointed in finding gin as dear as ever—for which he had little to regret for he prefered good ale to any spirits   and now the Malt and beer tax is in full cry what is the poor man to expect   it may benefit the farmers a little and the common brewers a good deal and there no doubt the matter will end   the poor man will not find the refuse of any more use to him then a dry bone to a hungry dog—excuse the simile reader for the poor have been likened unto dogs before now   and many other of these time serving hue and cries might be noticed in which the poor man was promised as much benefit as the stork was in the fable for pulling out the bone from the Wolfs throat and who got just as much at last as the stork did for his pains

some of the patriots of these meetings seem to consider the corn law as a bone sticking in the throat of the countrys distress but I am sure that the poor man will be no better off in such a matter—he will only be 'burning his fingers' and not filling his belly by harbouring any notions of benefit from that quarter for he is so many degrees lower in the Thremometer of distress that such benefits to others will not reach him and tho the Farmers should again be in their summer splendour of 'high prices' and 'better markets' as they phrase it the poor man would still be found very little above freezing point— at least I very much fear so for I speak from experience and not from hearsay and hopes as some do   some years back when grain sold at 5 and 6 guineas a quarter I can point out a many villages where the Farmers under a combination for each others inter[e]sts would give no more in winter then 10 shillings per Week   I will not say that all did so for in a many places and at that very time Farmers whose good intentions was 'to live and let live' gave from 12 to 15 shillings per

week and these men would again do the same thing but they could
not compel others and there it is were the poor man looses the benefit
that ought to fall to him from the farmers 'better markets' and 'high
prices' for corn   I hope Mr Editor that I do not offend by my plain
speaking for I wish only to be satisfied about these few particulars
and I am so little of a politician that I would rather keep out of the
crowd then that my hobnails should trample on the gouty toes of
any one   tho I cannot help thinking when I read your paper that
there is a vast number of taxable advocates wearing barrack shoes or
they would certainly not leave the advocates for reform to acchieve
their triumphs without a struggle   I wish the good of the people may
be found at the end and that in the general triumph the poor man
may not be forgotten   for the poor have many oppressors and no
voice to be heard above them   he is a dumb burthen in the scorn of
the worlds prosperity yet in its adversity they are found ever ready
to aid and assist and tho that be but as the widows mite yet his
honest feelings in the cause are as worthy as the orators proudest
orations   Being a poor man myself I am naturally wishing to see
some one become the advocate and champion for the poor not in his
speeches but his actions   for speeches are now adays nothing but
words and sound   Politicians are known to be exceedingly wise as far
as regards themselves and we have heard of one who tho his whole
thoughts seemd constantly professing the good of his country yet he
was cunning enough to keep one thought to himself in the hour of
danger when he luckily hit upon the thought of standing upon his hat
to keep himself from catching cold not to die for the good of the
country as some others did and to be alive as he is at this moment
now if the poor mans chance at these meetings is any thing better
then being a sort of foot cushion for the benefit of others I shall be
exceedingly happy but as it is I much fear it as the poor mans lot
seems to have been so long remembered as to be entirely forgotten
                                   I am sir your humble Servant
                                            A Poor Man

                          ᕧᕧᕧ

Remembrances

SUMMERS pleasures they are gone like to visions every one
And the cloudy days of autumn and of winter cometh on
I tried to call them back but unbidden they are gone
Far away from heart and eye and for ever far away
Dear heart and can it be that such raptures meet decay
I thought them all eternal when by Langley bush I lay
I thought them joys eternal when I used to shout and play
On its banks at clink and bandy chock* and taw and ducking
   stone*
Where silence sitteth now on the wild heath as her own
Like a ruin of the past all alone

When I used to lye and sing by old eastwells boiling spring
When I used to tie the willow boughs together for a swing
And fish with crooked pins and thread and never catch a thing
With heart just like a feather—now as heavy as a stone
When beneath old lea close oak I the bottom branches broke
To make our harvest cart like so many working folk
And then to cut a straw at the brook to have a soak
O I never dreamed of parting or that trouble had a sting
Or that pleasures like a flock of birds would ever take to wing
Leaving nothing but a little naked spring

When jumping time away on old cross berry way
And eating awes* like sugar plumbs ere they had lost the may
And skipping like a leveret before the peep of day
On the rolly poly up and down of pleasant Swordy well
When in round oaks narrow lane as the south got black again
We sought the hollow ash that was shelter from the rain
With our pockets full of pease we had stolen from the grain
How delicious was the dinner time on such a showery day
O words are poor reciepts* for what time hath stole away
The ancient pulpit trees and the play

When for school oer little field with its brook and wooden brig
Where I swaggered like a man though I was not half so big
While I held my little plough though twas but a willow twig
And drove my team along made of nothing but a name

'Gee hep' and 'hoit' and 'woi'—O I never call to mind
Those pleasant names of places but I leave a sigh behind
While I see the little mouldiwarps* hang sweeing to the wind
On the only aged willow that in all the field remains
And nature hides her face while theyre sweeing in their chains
And in a silent murmuring complains

Here was commons for their hills where they seek for freedom
    still
Though every commons gone and though traps are set to kill
The little homeless miners—O it turns my bosom chill
When I think of old 'sneap green' puddocks nook and hilly snow
Where bramble bushes grew and the daisey gemmed in dew
And the hills of silken grass like to cushions on the view
Where we threw the pismire* crumbs when we'd nothing else
    to do
All leveled like a desert by the never weary plough
All banished like the sun where that cloud is passing now
And settled here for ever on its brow

O I never thought that joys would run away from boys
Or that boys should change their minds and forsake mid-summer
    joys
But alack I never dreamed that the world had other toys
To petrify first feelings like the fable into stone
Till I found the pleasure past and a winter come at last
Then the fields were sudden bare and the sky got over cast
And boy hoods pleasing haunts like a blossom in the blast
Was shrivelled to a withered weed and trampled down and done
Till vanished was the morning spring and set the summer sun
And winter fought her battle strife and won

By Langley bush I roam but the bush hath lefts its hill
On cowper green I stray tis a desert strange and chill
And spreading lea close oak ere decay had penned its will
To the axe of the spoiler and self interest fell a prey
And crossberry way and old round oaks narrow lane
With its hollow trees like pulpits I shall never see again
Inclosure like a buonaparte let not a thing remain

It levelled every bush and tree and levelled every hill
And hung the moles for traitors—though the brook is running
    still
It runs a naked stream cold and chill

O had I known as then joy had left the paths of men
I had watched her night and day besure and never slept agen
And when she turned to go O I'd caught her mantle then
And wooed her like a lover by my lonely side to stay
Aye knelt and worshiped on as love in beautys bower
And clung upon her smiles as a bee upon a flower
And gave her heart my poesys all cropt in a sunny hour
As keepsakes and pledges all to never fade away
But love never heeded to treasure up the may
So it went the common road to decay

The Flitting

I VE left my own old home of homes
Green fields and every pleasant place
The summer like a stranger comes
I pause and hardly know her face
I miss the hazels happy green
The blue bells quiet hanging blooms
Where envy's sneer was never seen
Where staring malice never comes

I miss the heath its yellow furze
Molehills and rabbit tracks that lead
Through beesom ling and teazel burrs
That spread a wilderness indeed
The woodland oaks and all below
That their white powdered branches shield
The mossy pads*—the very crow
Croaked music in my native fields

I sit me in my corner chair
That seems to feel itself from home
I hear bird music here and there
From awthorn hedge and orchard come

I hear but all is strange and new
—I sat on my old bench in June
The sailing puddocks* shrill 'peelew'
Oer royce wood seemed a sweeter tune

I walk adown the narrow lane
The nightingale is singing now
But like to me she seems at loss
For royce wood and its shielding bough
I lean upon the window sill
The trees and summer happy seem
Green sunny green they shine—but still
My heart goes far away to dream

Of happiness and thoughts arise
With home bred pictures many a one
Green lanes that shut out burning skies
And old crooked stiles to rest upon
Above them hangs the maple tree
Below grass swells a velvet hill
And little footpads sweet to see
Goes seeking sweeter places still

With bye and bye a brook to cross
Oer which a little arch is thrown
No brook is here I feel the loss
From home and friends and all alone
—The stone pit with its shelving sides
Seemed hanging rocks in my esteem
I miss the prospect far and wide
From Langley bush and so I seem

Alone and in a stranger scene
Far from spots my heart esteems
The closen with their ancient green
Heath woods and pastures sunny streams
The hawthorns here were hung with may
But still they seem in deader green
The sun een seems to lose its way
Nor knows the quarter it is in

I dwell on trifles like a child
I feel as ill becomes a man
And still my thoughts like weedlings wild
Grow up to blossom where they can
They turn to places known so long
And feel that joy was dwelling there
So homebred pleasure fills the song
That has no present joys to heir

I read in books for happiness
But books mistake the way to joy
They change—as well give age the glass
To hunt its visage when a boy
For books they follow fashions new
And throw all old esteems away
In crowded streets flower never grew
But many there hath died away

Some sing the pomps of chivalry
As legends of the ancient time
Where gold and pearls and mystery
Are shadows painted for sublime
But passions of sublimity
Belong to plain and simpler things
And David underneath a tree
Sought when a shepherd Salems springs

Where moss did unto cushions spring
Forming a seat of velvet hue
A small unnoticed trifling thing
To all but heavens hailing dew
And Davids crown hath passed away
Yet poesy breaths his shepherd-skill
His palace lost and to this day
The little moss is blooming still

Strange scenes mere shadows are to me
Vague unpersonifying things
I love with my old hants* to be
By quiet woods and gravel springs

Where little pebbles wear as smooth
As hermits beads by gentle floods
Whose noises doth my spirits sooth
And warms them into singing moods

Here every tree is strange to me
All foreign things where ere I go
Theres none where boyhood made a swee
Or clambered up to rob a crow
No hollow tree or woodland bower
Well known when joy was beating high
Where beauty ran to shun a shower
And love took pains to keep her dry

And laid the shoaf* upon the ground
To keep her from the dripping grass
And ran for stowks* and set them round
Till scarce a drop of rain could pass
Through—where the maidens they reclined
And sung sweet ballads now forgot
Which brought sweet memorys to the mind
But here no memory knows them not

There have I sat by many a tree
And leaned oer many a rural stile
And conned my thoughts as joys to me
Nought heeding who might frown or smile
Twas natures beautys that inspired
My heart with rapture not its own
And shes a fame that never tires
How could I feel myself alone

No—pasture molehills used to lie
And talk to me of sunny days
And then the glad sheep resting bye
All still in ruminating praise
Of summer and the pleasant place
And every weed and blossom too
Was looking upward in my face
With friendship welcome 'how do ye do'

All tennants of an ancient place
And heirs of noble heritage
Coeval they with adams race
And blest with more substantial age
For when the world first saw the sun
These little flowers beheld him too
And when his love for earth begun
They were the first his smiles to woo

These little lambtoe bunches springs
In red tinged and begolden dye
For ever and like china kings
They come but never seem to die
These may-blooms with its little threads
Still comes upon the thorny bowers
And neer forgets those pinky heads
Like fairy pins amid the flowers

And still they bloom as in the day
They first crowned wilderness and rock
When abel haply crowned with may
The firstlings of his little flock
And Eve might from the matted thorn
To deck her lone and lovely brow
Reach that same rose that heedless scorn
Misnames as the dog rosey now

Give me no high flown fangled things
No haughty pomp in marching chime
Where muses play on golden strings
And splendour passes for sublime
Where citys stretch as far as fame
And fancys straining eye can go
And piled untill the sky for shame
Is stooping far away below

I love the verse that mild and bland
Breaths of green fields and open sky
I love the muse that in her hand
Bears wreaths of native poesy

Who walks nor skips the pasture brook
In scorn—but by the drinking horse
Leans oer its little brig to look
How far the sallows lean accross

And feels a rapture in her breast
Upon their root-fringed grains to mark
A hermit morehens sedgy nest
Just like a naiads summer bark
She counts the eggs she cannot reach
Admires the spot and loves it well
And yearns so natures lessons teach
Amid such neighbourhoods to dwell

I love the muse who sits her down
Upon the molehills little lap
Who feels no fear to stain her gown
And pauses by the hedgerow gap
Not with that affectation praise
Of song to sing and never see
A field flower grow in all her days
Or een a forests aged tree

Een here my simple feelings nurse
A love for every simple weed
And een this little shepherds purse
Grieves me to cut it up—Indeed
I feel at times a love and joy
For every weed and every thing
A feeling kindred from a boy
A feeling brought with every spring

And why—this 'shepherds purse' that grows
In this strange spot in days gone bye
Grew in the little garden rows
Of my old home now left—and I
Feel what I never felt before
This weed an ancient neighbour here
And though I own the spot no more
Its every trifle makes it dear

The ivy at the parlour end
The woodbine at the garden gate
Are all and each affections friend
That renders parting desolate
But times will change and friends must part
And nature still can make amends
Their memory lingers round the heart
Like life whose essence is its friends .

Time looks on pomp with careless moods
Or killing apathys disdain
—So where old marble citys stood
Poor persecuted weeds remain
She feels a love for little things
That very few can feel beside
And still the grass eternal springs
Where castles stood and grandeur died

Decay

O POESY is on the wane
For fancys visions all unfitting
I hardly know her face again
Nature herself seems on the flitting
The fields grow old and common things
The grass the sky the winds a blowing
And spots where still a beauty clings
Are sighing 'going all a going'
O poesy is on the wane
I hardly know her face again

The bank with brambles over spread
And little molehills round about it
Was more to me then laurel shades
With paths and gravel finely clouted*
And streaking here and streaking there
Through shaven grass and many a border
With rutty lanes had no compare
And heaths were in a richer order

But poesy is in its wane
I hardly know her face again

I sat with love by pasture stream
Aye beautys self was sitting bye
Till fields did more then edens seem
Nor could I tell the reason why
I often drank when not a dry
To pledge her health in draught divine
Smiles made it nectar from the sky
Love turned een water into wine
O poesy is on the wane
I cannot find her face again

The sun those mornings used to find
When clouds were other-country-mountains
And heaven looked upon the mind
With groves and rocks and mottled fountains
These heavens are gone—the mountains grey
Turned mist—the sun a homeless ranger
Pursues a naked weary way
Unnoticed like a very stranger
O poesy is on its wane
Nor love nor joy is mine again

Loves sun went down without a frown
For every joy it used to grieve us
I often think that west is gone
Ah cruel time to undeceive us
The stream it is a naked stream
Where we on sundays used to ramble
The sky hangs oer a broken dream
The brambles dwindled to a bramble
O poesy is on its wane
I cannot find her haunts again

Mere withered stalks and fading trees
And pastures spread with hills and rushes
Are all my fading vision sees
Gone gone is raptures flooding gushes

When mushrooms they were fairy bowers
Their marble pillars overswelling
And danger paused to pluck the flowers
That in their swarthy rings were dwelling
But poesys spells are on the wane
Nor joy nor fear is mine again

Aye poesy hath passed away
And fancys visions undecieve us
The night hath taen the place of day
And why should passing shadows grieve us
I thought the flowers upon the hills
Were flowers from Adams open gardens
And I have had my summer thrills
And I have had my hearts rewardings
So poesy is on the wane
I hardly know her face again

And friendship it hath burned away
Just like a very ember cooling
A make believe on april day
That sent the simple heart a fooling
Mere jesting in an earnest way
Decieving on and still decieving
And hope is but a fancy play
And joy the art of true believing
For poesy is on the wane
O could I feel her faith again

⁓⁓⁓

Journey out of Essex

JULY 18—1841—Sunday   Felt very melancholly—went a walk on
the forest in the afternoon—fell in with some gipseys one of whom
offered to assist in my escape from the mad house by hideing me in
his camp to which I almost agreed but told him I had no money to
start with but if he would do so I would promise him fifty pounds

and he agreed to do so before saturday   on friday I went again but he did not seem so willing so I said little about it—On Sunday I went and they were all gone—an old wide awake hat and an old straw bonnet of the plumb pudding sort was left behind—and I put the hat in my pocket thinking it might be usefull for another opper-tunity   as good luck would have it, it turned out to be so

July 19—Monday   Did nothing

July 20—Reconnitered the rout the Gipsey pointed out and found it a legible one to make a movement and having only honest courage and myself in my army I led the way and my troops soon followed but being careless in mapping down the rout as the Gipsey told me I missed the lane to Enfield town and was going down Enfield highway till I passed 'The Labour in vain' Public house where a person I knew comeing out of the door told me the way

I walked down the lane gently and was soon in Enfield Town and bye and bye on the great York Road where it was all plain sailing and stearing ahead meeting no enemy and fearing none I reached Steven-age where being Night I got over a gate crossed over the corner of a green paddock where seeing a pond or hollow in the corner I forced to stay off a respectable distance to keep from falling into it for my legs were nearly knocked up and began to stagger   I scaled some old rotten paleings into the yard and then had higher pailings to clamber over to get into the shed or hovel which I did with diffi-culty being rather weak   to my good luck I found some trusses of clover piled up about 6 or more feet square which I gladly mounted and slept on   there was some trays in the hovel on which I could have reposed had I not found a better bed   I slept soundly but had a very uneasy dream   I thought my first wife lay on my left arm and some-body took her away from my side which made me wake up rather unhappy   I thought as I awoke somebody said 'Mary' but nobody was near—I lay down with my head towards the north to show my self the steering point in the morning

July 21—when I awoke daylight was looking in on every side and fearing my garrison might be taken by storm and myself be made prisoner I left my lodging by the way I got in and thanked God for his kindness in procureing it (for any thing in a famine is better than nothing and any place that giveth the weary rest is a blessing)   I gained the north road again and steered due north—on the left hand side the road under the bank like a cave I saw a Man and boy coiled up asleep which I hailed and they woke up to tell me the name of the next village[1]

Some where on the London side the 'Plough' Public house a Man passed me on horseback in a Slop frock and said 'here's another of the broken down haymakers' and threw me a penny to get a half pint of beer which I picked up and thanked him for and when I got to the plough I called for a half pint and drank it and got a rest and escaped a very heavy shower in the bargain by having a shelter till it was over —afterwards I would have begged a penny of two drovers who were very saucey so I begged no more of any body meet who I would

I passed 3 or 4 good built houses on a hill and a public house on the road side in the hollow below them I seemed to pass the Milestones very quick in the morning but towards night they seemed to be stretched further asunder   I got to a village further on and forgot the name   the road on the left hand was quite over shaded by some trees and quite dry so I sat down half an hour and made a good many wishes for breakfast but wishes was no hearty meal so I got up as hungry as I sat down—I forget here the names of the villages I passed through but recollect at late evening going through Potton in Bedfordshire where I called in a house to light my pipe in which was a civil old woman and a young country wench making lace on a cushion as round as a globe and a young fellow all civil people—I asked them a few questions as to the way and where the clergyman and overseer lived but they scarcely heard me or gave me no answer[2]

I then went through Potton and happened with a kind talking country man who told me the Parson lived a good way from where

[1] Baldeck [Clare's footnote; i.e. Baldock].
[2] Note. On searching my pockets after the above was written I found part of a newspaper vide 'Morning Chronicle' on which the following fragments were pencilled   soon after I got the information from labourers going to work or travellers journeying along to better their condition as I was hoping to do mine   in fact I believed I saw home in every ones countenance which seemed so cheerful in my own—'There is no place like home' the following was written by the Roadside:—

1st Day—Tuesday started from Enfield and slept at Stevenage on some
          clover trusses—cold lodging
Wednesday—Jacks Hill is passed already consisting of a beer shop and
          some houses on the hill appearing newly built—the last Mile
          stone 35 Miles from London   got through Baldeck and sat under
          a dry hedge and had a rest in lieu of breakfast.

I was or overseer I do'n't know which so I went on hopping with a crippled foot for a gravel had got into my old shoes one of which had now nearly lost the sole. Had I found the overseers house at hand or the Parsons I should have gave my name and begged for a shilling to carry me home but I was forced to brush on penny less and be thankfull I had a leg to move on—I then asked him wether he could tell me of a farm yard any where on the road where I could find a shed and some dry straw and he said yes and if you will go with me I will show you the place—its a public house on the left hand side the road at the sign of the 'Ram' but seeing a stone or flint heap I longed to rest as one of my feet was very painfull so I thanked him for his kindness and bid him go on—but the good natured fellow lingered awhile as if wishing to conduct me and then suddenly reccolecting that he had a hamper on his shoulder and a lock up bag in his hand cram full to meet the coach which he feared missing—he started hastily and was soon out of sight—I followed looking in vain for the countrymans straw bed—and not being able to meat it I lay down by a shed side under some Elm trees between the wall and the trees being a thick row planted some 5 or 6 feet from the buildings   I lay there and tried to sleep but the wind came in between them so cold that I lay till I quaked like the ague and quitted the lodging for a better at the Ram which I could hardly hope to find—It now began to grow dark apace and the odd houses on the road began to light up and show the inside tennants lots very comfortable and my outside lot very uncomfortable and wretched—still I hobbled forward as well as I could and at last came to the Ram   the shutters were not closed and the lighted window looked very cheering but I had no money and did not like to go in   there was a sort of shed or gighouse at the end but I did not like to lie there as the people were up—so I still travelled on   the road was very lonely and dark in places being overshadowed with trees   at length I came to a place where the road branched off into two turnpikes one to the right about and the other straight forward and on going bye my eye glanced on a mile stone standing under the hedge so I heedlessly turned back to read it to see where the other road led too and on doing so I found it led to London   I then suddenly forgot which was North or South and though I narrowly examined both ways I could see no tree or bush or stone heap that I could reccolect I had passed so I went on mile after mile almost convinced I was going the same way I came and these thoughts were so strong upon me that doubt and hopelessness made me turn so feeble that I was scarcely able to walk yet I could not sit down or give up but shuffled along till I saw a lamp shining as bright as the moon which on nearing I found was suspended over a Tollgate[1] before I got through the man came out with a candle and eyed me narrowly but having no fear I stopt to ask him wether I was going northward and he said when you get through the gate you are; so I thanked him kindly and went through on the other side and gathered my old strength as my doubts vanished I soon cheered up and hummed the air of Highland Mary as I went on I at length fell in with an odd house all alone near a wood but I could not see what the sign was though the sign seemed to stand oddly enough in a sort of trough or spout there was a large porch over the door and being weary I crept in and glad enough I was to find I could lye with my legs straight the inmates were all gone to roost for I could hear them turn over in bed as I lay at full length on the stones in the porch—I slept here till daylight and I felt very much refreshed as I got up—I blest my two wives and both their familys when I lay down and when I got up and when I thought of some former difficultys on a like occasion I could not help blessing the Queen[2] Having passed a Lodge on the left hand within a mile and half or less of a town I think it might be[3] St. Ives but I forget the name I sat down to rest on a flint heap where I might rest half an hour or more and while sitting here I saw a tall Gipsey come out of the Lodge gate and make down the road towards where I was sitting when she got up to me on seeing she was a young woman with an honest looking countenance rather handsome

[1] [There was a Turnpike Gate at Temsford or Tamesford or Tempsford, four miles and six furlongs south of St. Neots.]

[2] MS. 8, p. 25, contains the following note, written in a very disordered hand which was due in all probability to a conjunction of fatigue and emotional agitation:

The man whose daughter is the queen of England is now sitting on a stone heap on the highway to bugden without a farthing in his pocket and without eating a bit of food ever since yesterday morning—when he was offered a bit of Bread and cheese at Enfield—he has not had any since but If I put a little fresh speed on hope too may speed tomorrow—O Mary mary If you knew how anxious I am to see you and dear Patty with the children I think you would come and meet me

[This was presumably written late on Wednesday, 21st. Bugden was an accepted variant of Buckden.]

[3] It was St. Neots [Clare's footnote].

I spoke to her and asked her a few questions which she answered readily and with evident good humour so I got up and went on to the next town with her—she cautioned me on the way to put somthing in my hat to keep the crown up and said in a lower tone 'you'll be noticed' but not knowing what she hinted—I took no notice and made no reply   at length she pointed to a small tower church which she called Shefford Church and advised me to go on a footway which would take me direct to it and I should shorten my journey fifteen miles by doing so   I would gladly have taken the young womans advice feeling that it was honest and a nigh guess towards the truth but fearing I might loose my way and not be able to find the north road again I thanked her and told her I should keep to the road when she bade me 'good day' and went into a house or shop on the left hand side the road   I have but a slight reccolection of my journey between here and Stilton for I was knocked up and noticed little or nothing—one night I lay in a dyke bottom from the wind and went sleep half an hour when I suddenly awoke and found one side wet through from the sock in the dyke bottom so I got out and went on—I remember going down a very dark road hung over with trees on both sides very thick which seemed to extend a mile or two   I then entered a town and some of the chamber windows had candle lights shineing in them—I felt so weary here I forced to sit down on the ground to rest myself and while I sat here a Coach that seemed to be heavy laden came rattling up and stopt in the hollow below me and I cannot reccolect its ever passing by me[1]   I then got up and pushed onward seeing little to notice for the road very often looked as stupid as myself and I was very often half asleep as I went   on the third day I satisfied my hunger by eating the grass by the road side which seemed to taste something like bread   I was hungry and eat heartily till I was satisfied and in fact the meal seemed to do me good   the next and last day I reccolected that I had some tobacco and my box of lucifers being exausted I could not light my pipe so I took to chewing Tobacco all day and eat the quids when I had done and I was never hungry afterwards—I remember passing through Buckden and going a length of road afterwards but I dont reccolect the name of any place untill I came to stilton where I was compleatly foot

[1] Clare's marginal note: The Coach did pass me as I sat under some trees by a high wall and the chips flew hard in my face and wakened me up from a doze when I knocked the gravel out of my shoes and started.

foundered and broken down   when I had got about half way through the town a gravel causeway invited me to rest myself so I lay down and nearly went sleep   a young woman (so I guessed by the voice) came out of a house and said 'poor creature' and another more elderly said 'O he shams' but when I got up the latter said 'o no he dont' as I hobbled along very lame   I heard the voices but never looked back to see where they came from—when I got near the Inn at the end of the gravel walk I meet two young women and I asked one of them wether the road branching to the right by the end of the Inn[1] did not lead to Peterborough and she said 'Yes' it did so as soon as ever I was on it I felt myself in homes way and went on rather more cheerfull though I forced to rest oftener then usual   before I got to Peterborough a man and woman passed me in a cart and on hailing me as they passed I found they were neighbours from Helpstone where I used to live—I told them I was knocked up which they could easily see and that I had neither eat or drank anything since I left Essex   when I told my story they clubbed together and threw me fivepence out of the cart   I picked it up and called at a small public house near the bridge were I had two half pints of ale and two-penn'rth of bread and cheese   when I had done I started quite refreshed only my feet was more crippled then ever and I could scarcely make a walk of it over the stones and being half ashamed to sit down in the street I forced to keep on the move and got through Peterborough better then I expected   when I got on the high road I rested on the stone heaps as I passed till I was able to go on afresh and bye and bye I passed Walton and soon reached Werrington and was making for the Beehive[2] as fast as I could when a cart met me with a man and woman and a boy in it when nearing me the woman jumped out and caught fast hold of my hands and wished me to get into the cart but I refused and thought her either drunk or mad but when I was told it was my second wife Patty I got in and was soon at Northborough   but Mary was not there neither could I get any information about her further then the old story of her being dead six years ago which might be taken from a bran new old Newspaper printed a dozen years ago but I took no notice of the blarney having seen her myself about a twelve month ago alive and well and as

[1] i.e. at Norman Cross, 5¾ miles to Peterborough.
[2] Whellan's *Directory*, 1849, mentions only the *Cock*, the *Blue Bell*, the *Wheat Sheaf*, and the *Three Horse Shoes*.

young as ever—so here I am homeless at home and half gratified to
feel that I can be happy anywhere

> May none those marks of my sad fate efface
> For they appeal from tyranny to God
>   Byron

July 24—1841—Returned home out of Essex and found no Mary—
her and her family are nothing to me now though she herself was
once the dearest of all—and how can I forget

From *Child Harold*

Now melancholly autumn comes anew
With showery clouds and fields of wheat tanned brown
Along the meadow banks I peace pursue
And see the wild flowers gleaming up and down
Like sun and light—the ragworts golden crown
Mirrors like sunshine when sunbeams retire
And silver yarrow—there's the little town
And oer the meadows gleams that slender spire
Reminding me of one—and waking fond desire

I love thee nature in my inmost heart
Go where I will thy truth seems from above
Go where I will thy landscape forms a part
Of heaven—e'en these fens where wood nor grove
Are seen—their very nakedness I love
For one dwells nigh that secret hopes prefer
Above the race of women—like the dove
I mourn her abscence—fate that would deter
My hate for all things—strengthens love for her

Thus saith the great and high and lofty one
Whose name is holy—home eternity
In the high and holy place I dwell alone
And with them also that I wish to see
Of contrite humble spirits—from sin free

Who tremble at my word—and good receive
—Thou high and lofty one—O give to me
Truths low estate and I will glad believe
If such I am not—such I'm feign to live

That form from boyhood loved and still loved on
That voice—that look—that face of one delight
Loves register for years, months, weeks—time past and gone
Her looks was ne'er forgot or out of sight
—Mary the muse of every song I write
Thy cherished memory never leaves my own
Though cares chill winter doth my manhood blight
And freeze like Niobe my thoughts to stone—
Our lives are two—our end and aim is one

.   .   .   .   .

Tis pleasant now days hours begin to pass
To dewy Eve—To walk down narrow close
And feel ones feet among refreshing grass
And hear the insects in their homes discourse
And startled blackbird flye from covert close
Of white thorn hedge with wild fears fluttering wings
And see the spire and hear the clock toll hoarse
And whisper names—and think oer many things
That love hurds up* in truths imaginings

Fame blazed upon me like a comets glare
Fame waned and left me like a fallen star
Because I told the evil what they are
And truth and falshood never wished to mar
My Life hath been a wreck—and I've gone far
For peace and truth—and hope—for home and rest
—Like Edens gates—fate throws a constant bar—
Thoughts may o'ertake the sunset in the west
—Man meets no home within a womans breast

Though they are blazoned in the poets song
As all the comforts which our lifes contain
I read and sought such joys my whole life long
And found the best of poets sung in vain

But still I read and sighed and sued again
And lost no purpose where I had the will
I almost worshiped when my toils grew vain
Finding no antidote my pains to kill
I sigh a poet and a lover still

Song

Dying gales of sweet even
How can you sigh so
Though the sweet day is leaving
And the sun sinketh low
How can you sigh so
For the wild flower is gay
And her dew gems all glow
For the abscence of day

Dying gales of sweet even
Breath music from toil
Dusky eve is loves heaven
And meets beautys smile
Love leans on the stile
Where the rustic brooks flow
Dying gales all the while
How can you sigh so

Dying gales round a prison
To fancy may sigh
But day here hath risen
Over prospects of joy
Here Mary would toy
When the sun it got low
Even gales whisper joy
And never sigh so

Labour lets man his brother
Retire to his rest
The babe meets its mother
And sleeps on her breast—

The sun in the west
Has gone down in the ocean
Dying gales gently sweep
O'er the hearts ruffled motion
And sing it to sleep

Song

No single hour can stand for nought
No moment hand can move
But calenders a aching thought
Of my first lonely love

Where silence doth the loudest call
My secrets to betray
As moonlight holds the night in thrall
As suns reveal the day

I hide it in the silent shades
Till silence finds a tongue
I make its grave where time invades
Till time becomes a song

I bid my foolish heart be still
But hopes will not be chid
My heart will beat—and burn—and chill
First love will not be hid

When summer ceases to be green
And winter bare and blea—
Death may forget what I have been
But I must cease to be

When words refuse before the crowd
My Marys name to give
The muse in silence sings aloud
And there my love will live

Now harvest smiles embrowning all the plain
The sun of heaven oer its ripeness shines
'Peace-plenty' has been sung nor sung in vain
As all bring forth the makers grand designs

—Like gold that brightens in some hidden mines
His nature is the wealth that brings increase
To all the world—his sun forever shines
—He hides his face and troubles they increase
He smiles—the sun looks out in wealth and peace

This life is made of lying and grimace
This world is filled with whoring and decieving
Hypocrisy ne'er masks an honest face
Story's are told—but seeing is believing
And I've seen much from which there's no retrieving
I've seen deception take the place of truth
I've seen knaves flourish—and the country grieving
Lies was the current gospel in my youth
And now a man—I'm further off from truth

I am

I AM—yet what I am, none cares or knows;
　　My friends forsake me like a memory lost:
I am the self-consumer of my woes—
　　They rise and vanish in oblivions host,
Like shadows in love frenzied stifled throes
　　And yet I am, and live—like vapours tost

Into the nothingness of scorn and noise,
　　Into the living sea of waking dreams,
Where there is neither sense of life or joys,
　　But the vast shipwreck of my lifes esteems;
Even the dearest that I love the best
　　Are strange—nay, rather, stranger than the rest.

I long for scenes where man hath never trod
　　A place where woman never smiled or wept
There to abide with my Creator God,
　　And sleep as I in childhood sweetly slept,
Untroubling and untroubled where I lie
　　The grass below, above, the vaulted sky.

Sonnet: 'I Am'

I FEEL I am, I only know I am
And plod upon the earth as dull and void
Earth's prison chilled my body with its dram
Of dullness, and my soaring thoughts destroyed.
I fled to solitudes from passions dream
But strife persued—I only know I am.
I was a being created in the race
Of men disdaining bounds of place and time—
A spirit that could travel o'er the space
Of earth and heaven—like a thought sublime,
Tracing creation, like my maker, free—
A soul unshackled like eternity,
Spurning earth's vain and soul debasing thrall
But now I only know I am—that's all.

Song

I WISH I was where I would be
With love alone to dwell
Was I but her or she but me
Then love would all be well
I wish to send my thoughts to her
As quick as thoughts can fly
But as the wind the waters stir
The mirrors change and flye

An invite to Eternity

WILT thou go with me sweet maid
Say maiden wilt thou go with me
Through the valley depths of shade
Of night and dark obscurity
Where the path hath lost its way
Where the sun forgets the day
Where there's nor life nor light to see
Sweet maiden wilt thou go with me

Where stones will turn to flooding streams
Where plains will rise like ocean waves
Where life will fade like visioned dreams
And mountains darken into caves
Say maiden wilt thou go with me
Through this sad non-identity
Where parents live and are forgot
And sisters live and know us not

Say maiden wilt thou go with me
In this strange death of life to be
To live in death and be the same
Without this life or home or name
At once to be and not to be
That was and is not—yet to see
Things pass like shadows—and the sky
Above, below, around us lie.

The land of shadows wilt thou trace
And look nor know each others face
The present mixed with reasons gone
And past and present all as one
Say maiden can thy life be led
To join the living with the dead
Then trace thy footsteps on with me
We're wed to one eternity

Sonnet

POETS love nature and themselves are love;
The scorn of fools and mock of idle pride
The vile in nature worthless deeds approve
They court the vile and spurn all good beside
Poets love nature like the calm of heaven
Her gifts like heaven's love spread far and wide
In all her works there are no signs of leaven
Sorrow abashes from her simple pride
Her flowers like pleasures have their seasons birth
And bloom through regions here below

They are her very scriptures upon earth
And teach us simple mirth where e'er we go
Even in prison they can solace me
For where they bloom God is, and I am free.

A Vision

I LOST the love of heaven above
I spurned the lust of earth below
I felt the sweets of fancied love
And hell itself my only foe

I lost earth's joys but felt the glow
Of heaven's flame abound in me
Till loveliness and I did grow
The bard of immortality

I loved but woman fell away
I hid me from her faded fame
I snatched the sun's eternal ray
And wrote till earth was but a name

In every language upon earth
On every shore, o'er every sea,
I gave my name immortal birth,
And kept my spirit with the free
                              August 2nd 1844

Song

I HID my love when young while* I
Coudn't bear the buzzing of a flye
I hid my love to my despite
Till I could not bear to look at light
I dare not gaze upon her face
But left her memory in each place
Where ere I saw a wild flower lye
I kissed and bade my love good bye

I met her in the greenest dells
Where dew drops pearl the wood blue bells
The lost breeze kissed her bright blue eye
The bee kissed and went singing bye
A sun beam found a passage there
A gold chain round her neck so fair
As secret as the wild bees song
She lay there all the summer long

I hid my love in field and town
Till e'en the breeze would knock me down
The Bees seemed singing ballads o'er
The flyes buss* turned a Lions roar
And even silence found a tongue
To haunt me all the summer long
The riddle nature could not prove
Was nothing else but secret love

Clock a Clay*

IN the cowslip's peeps I lye
Hidden from the buzzing fly
While green grass beneath me lies
Pearled wi' dew like fishes' eyes
Here I lie a Clock a clay
Waiting for the time o' day

While grassy forests quake surprise
And the wild wind sobs and sighs
My gold home rocks as like to fall
On its pillar green and tall
When the pattering rain drives bye
Clock a Clay keeps warm and dry

Day by day and night by night
All the week I hide from sight
In the cowslips peeps I lie
In rain and dew still warm and dry

Day and night and night and day
Red black spotted clock a clay

My home it shakes in wind and showers
Pale green pillar topt wi' flowers
Bending at the wild winds breath
Till I touch the grass beneath
Here still I live lone clock a clay
Watching for the time of day

[*Martinmass*]

T IS martinmass from rig to rig
Ploughed fields and meadow lands are blea
In hedge and field each restless twig
Is dancing on the naked tree
Flags in the dykes are bleached and brown
Docks by its sides are dry and dead
All but the ivy bows are brown
Upon each leaning dotterels head

Crimsoned with awes the awthorns bend
Oer meadows dykes and rising floods
The wild geese seek the reedy fen
And dark the storm comes oer the woods
The crowds of lapwings load the air
With buzes of a thousand wings
There flocks of sturnels too repair
When morning oer the valley springs

The crow sat on the willow

T HE Crow sat on the willow tree
A lifting up his wings
And glossy was his coat to see
And loud the ploughman sings

I love my love because I know
The milkmaid she loves me
And hoarsely croaked the glossy crow
Upon the willow tree
I love my love the ploughman sung
And all the field wi' music rung

I love my love a bonny lass
She keeps her pails so bright
And blythe she t[r]ips the dewy grass
At morning and at night
A cotton drab her morning gown
Her face was rosey health
She traced the pastures up and down
And nature was her wealth
He sung and turned each furrow down
His sweethearts love in cotton gown

My love is young and handsome
As any in the Town
She's worth a Ploughman's ransom
In the drab cotton gown
He sung and turned his furrows o'er
And urged his Team along
While on the willow as before
The old crow croaked his song
The ploughman sung his rustic Lay
And sung of Phebe all the day

The crow was in love no doubt
And wi a many things
The ploughman finished many a bout
And lustily he sings
My love she is a milking maid
Wi red and rosey cheek
O' cotton drab her gown was made
I loved her many a week
His milking maid the ploughman sung
Till all the fields around him rung

[*How hot the sun rushes*]

HOW hot the sun rushes
Like fire in the bushes
The wild flowers look sick at the foot of the tree
Birds nests are left lonely
The pewit sings only
And all seems disheartened, and lonely like me

Baked earth and burnt furrows
Where the rabbit he borrows
And yet it looks pleasant beneath the green tree
The crows nest look darkly
O'er fallows dried starkly
And the sheep all look restless as nature and me

Yet I love a meadow dwelling
Where nature is telling
A tale to the clear stream—its dearest to me
To sit in green shadows
While the herd turns to gadders
And runs from the hums of the fly and the bee

This spot is the fairest
The sweetest and rarest
This sweet sombre shade of the bright green tree
Where the morehens flag nest
On the waters calm breast
Lies near to this sweet spot thats been mother to me

Song

I'LL come to thee at even tide
When the west is streaked wi grey
I'll wish the night thy charms to hide
And daylight all away

I'll come to thee at set o' sun
Where white thorns i' the May
I'll come to thee when work is done
And love thee till the day

When Daisey stars are all turned green
And all is meadow grass
I'll wander down the bauk at e'en
And court the bonny Lass

The green banks and the rustleing sedge
I'll wander down at e'en
All slopeing to the waters edge
And in the water green

And theres the luscious meadow sweet
Beside the meadow drain
My lassie there I once did meet
Who I wish to meet again

The water lilies where in flower
The yellow and the white
I met her there at even's hour
And stood for half the night

We stood and loved in that green place
When sundays sun got low
Its beams reflected in her face
The fairest thing below

My sweet Ann Foot my bonny Ann
The Meadow banks are green
Meet me at even when you can
Be mine as you have been

GLOSSARY

a: On, as in 'a foot'; in, or at, as in 'a church'.

awe: Var. of *haw*.

ball: Ball, traditional name for an ox.

bandy: The knobbed stick used to strike the ball in games such as hockey. See *clink*.

bate: To teaze or worry. N.i.B. (i.e. not recorded by Baker).

bauk: Var. of *baulk*.

baulk: The unploughed strip between ploughed fields or furrows.

beavering hour: Time for refreshment, used especially of harvesting and haymaking.

bent: Coarse grass.

blea: Exposed and cold.

bottle of flags: A bundle of osiers or reeds. 'Bottle is also applied to a bundle of sticks collected from the hedges for firing.' The term is still used by thatchers.

brake: Fern.

breath: Var. of *breathe*.

brig: Var. of *bridge*.

brun-coloured: Bran-coloured.

brunny: Bran-coloured.

brunt: Wright gives 'to turn' or 'to stop', but in Clare the context suggests an abrupt or forceful movement. N.i.B.

brustle: To bustle about, make a great fuss or stir. N.i.B.

budget: A bag, pack, or wallet, generally of leather; especially a tinker's wallet and the pouch in which a mower carries his whetstone.

bumbarrel: The long-tailed tit.

burr: 1. *Verb*. To slow a wheel down by friction.
2. *Sub*. A halo round the moon, usually betokening rain.

buss: 1. A kiss.
2. A variant of *buzz*.

by times: Betimes.

cag: A small cask or keg. N.i.B.

checkering: Creating a pattern like that of a chequer or chessboard.

chelping: Chirping.

chickering: 'An imitative word expressive of the cricket's cry'. *Baker*.

chock: The game of marbles played by chocking or pitching marbles into a hole instead of shooting at a ring.

cirging: Surging. More likely to be the word in the manuscript than the weaker 'urging'.

clammed: Parched with thirst, or sometimes starved with hunger.

claum: In Wright, this occurs only as a verb, to seize or clutch with decided grasp. N.i.B.

clink: As in *clink and bandy chock*; 'clink' may be onomatopoeic, expressive of the contact of marble; alternatively, it may signify 'clench' in which case 'clink and bandy chock' may denote marbles played by first 'clenching' the thumb and then allowing it, on release, to strike the marble as the bandy or hockey stick strikes the ball.

clock: To clip-clop: onomatopoeic; N.i.B.

clock-a-clay: The lady-bird or lady-cow.

closen: The plural form of *close*.

clouted: Clothed or patched. Studded with large-headed nails.

clown: A rustic.

cotter: Var. of *cottager*.

courtseys: Curtseys. Shows the origin of the word from 'courteseys'.

covert: Cover't = cover it.

cowslap peeps: Cowslip eyes. Baker notes that the usual Northants. pronunciation was *keowslap*.

coyed: Decoyed.

crab: Crab apple.

crack: To boast or jest.

crane: As in 'act the crane': 'A man holds in his hand a long stick, with another tied at the top in the form of an L reversed, which represents the long neck and beak of the crane. This, with himself, is entirely covered with a large sheet. He mostly makes excellent sport, as he puts the whole company to the rout, picking out the young girls, and pecking at the bald heads of the old men . . .'. Clare's description in the Introduction to *The Village Minstrel*, 1821.

crank: Twisted, crooked. N.i.B.

crankle: To bend or wind.

crimped: Wrinkled, folded up.

crimping: A succession of small folds, frills or flutings.

crimpled: Wrinkled, crumpled.

crizzle: To crisp or crystallize; used of water that is beginning to freeze.

crizzling: Onomatopoeic use of the word, suggestive of gnawing.

cronk: To croak or honk, used especially of frogs and geese.

croodling: Contracting the body from cold, shrinking or huddling.

cross plumb skittles: Probably the game where there is (*a*) a cross, or support (stake or post); (*b*) a plumb-weight on a string attached to the cross-piece and allowed to swing and hit the skittles. N.i.B.

cross-row: Christ-cross-row = alphabet. Therefore 'as plain as the alphabet'.

crumping: Making a crunching sound, as frozen snow when it yields to the feet.

cucka ball: Cuckoo-ball; a light ball made of parti-coloured rags and flowers.

cuckoos: Various wild spring flowers such as Lady's Smock and Ragged Robin.

curdled: Clotted, as with irregularly textured bark.

cuts: Wood-cut illustrations.

dab: To strike.

dimute: Var. of *diminute*, diminished.

doll: Doll: traditional name for a milkmaid.

dotterel: A pollard-tree; 'old stumping trees in hedge rows, that are headed or lopped every ten or twelve years for fire-wood'. Clare.

douse: To soak or drench.

drabble: To slosh through mud; cf. Low German, *drabbeln*, to walk in water or mire.

drabbled: Draggled, smeared, muddied.

drowking: Drooping from drought.

ducking stone: 'Ducks' is a boys' game, played with three stones, surmounted by a fourth, which the player tries to dislodge by throwing at it from a short distance.

eke: To add to, to increase.

eldern: Pl. of elder.

elting: Soft, ploughed.

enarmoured: Var. of enamoured.

flaze: Flaring, as a candle when a current of air causes it to burn unsteadily.

flirt: To flit or flutter.

flusker: To fly with sudden motion, with an element of noise and commotion.

fodder: To feed.

fother: To feed.

fotherer: One who brings fodder.

foulroyce: Foul-rush, the dogwood or spindle-tree, i.e. either *Cornus sanguinea* or *Euonymus europaens*.

frail: Flail.

fret: To thaw.

frumitory: Frumenty, a dish made of hulled wheat boiled in milk and seasoned.

furze kidder: A person who collects and makes up bundles of furze, or furze-kids.

gadders: Restless movement, as of cows pestered by the gad-fly.

gadding: Moving in a restless, excited fashion.

gale: Breeze.

gangs: Goes.

gelid: Freezing cold; Clare may have learned this word from Thomson.

glabber: To jabber, chatter. Clare's use may well be metaphorical.

goss: Common furze, gorse.

gough: To gouge; cf. Clare's use of hugh for huge: also *sb.* gouge.

grain: A larger branch of a tree.

green-sickness: An anaemic disease mostly affecting young women about the age of puberty and giving a pale or greenish tinge to the complexion: *chlorosis*.

grubbed: Uprooted; the grub-axe was part axe and part hoe.

hants: Var. of *haunts*.

hariff: Var. of *hairif*, *hayrif*; cleavers or goose-grass, *Galium aparine*.

haynish: Wretched; cf. hayne [ME?]—a mean wretch, or niggard.

heir long: Heirloom.

hing: To hang.

hirkle: To crouch, to set up the back, as cattle who shrink from cold.

hirple: To limp.

hollow: Var. of *holler*, *holla*.

hugh: Clare's spelling of *huge*.

hurd up: To hoard.

huzzing: Clamorous, tumultuous.

icle: Icicle.

idless: Var. of *idleness*.

ingenious: Ingenuous, here ignorant.

jockolate: Var. of chocolate; a phonetic spelling.

Joe Millar: An old joke. Cf. *Joe Miller's Jest Book*, 5th edn., 1742.

joll: To walk lumberingly along.

knarl: To gnaw, nibble.

knewt: Newt.

land: An arable division of a furlong in an open field.

lare: To rest in a shelter.

ling: Heath; *Calluna vulgaris*.

list: To listen to.

loose: Clare's spelling of *lose*.

lown: Var. of *loon*.

lunge: To lurch, to hide, to skulk.

on the lurch: Lurking, in order to surprise.

majoram: Var. of marjoram, the aromatic herb.

mere mark: Meer: a strip or slip of grass land, serving as a boundary to different properties, or as a division of parishes in open fields.

mizardly: Miserly.

mizled: Wet with mizzle or drizzle.

morts: Great numbers.

mouldiwarp: The mole.

muscle: Clare's spelling of *mussel*.

nail passer: Corruption of nail-piecer: i.e. auger or gimlet.

near: Clare's spelling of *ne'er*.

nimble: To move nimbly.

oddling: One differing from the rest of a family, brood, or litter; generally applied to the smallest, or to one with a peculiarity.

oven house: Here the chiff-chaff or willow warbler occupies an oven-nest; Baker, however, attributes the oven-nest to the long-tailed titmouse.

pad: Var. of *path*.

pauled: Var. of palled.

pelt: To throw at.

pendil: Pendle-stone: a name given by quarry-men to the upper course in a stone-pit; in the quarries of Kingsthorpe, the hard blue stone was called the pendle-stone; used as a whetstone, especially for sharpening sickles and scythes.

pess: To soak; cf. piss.

pill: To peel or strip off.

pinder: A person employed to impound stray cattle.

pingle: A small enclosure, generally long and narrow.

pink: The chaffinch.

pismire: The ant.

platt: A flat stretch of ground.

pluft: Swollen, bloated, puffy; an epenthesis of *puffed*.

poesy: Clare's spelling of *posey*.

pooty: The girdled snail-shell: *Helix nemoralis*.

popples: Poplars.

prank: To adorn or decorate.

pranking: Frolicsome. N.i.B.

prevade: Var. of *pervade*.

prog: To poke or prod.

protentious: Portentous.

puddock: The name applied indiscriminately in Northants. to the fan-tail kite or buzzard and to the forked-tail kite.

pudge: A small puddle.

pudgy: Full of puddles.

quaking or quawking: Cawing.

ramp: To romp; to rampage; to grow luxuriantly.
rawky: Misty, foggy.
reak: To emit steam or vapour.
reciept: Recipe.
reek: Var. of *reak*.
ride: A riding: open space or road in a wood.
rig: Ridge.
rock: To sway, to walk unsteadily.
rotten: Rotten wood.
rout: Clare uses the same word for 'route' or 'rout' and therefore it
  seems to share a little of both senses wherever it occurs.

sallow: Species of *Salix*.
sawn: To saunter.
sawney: Idle.
scratt: Var. of *scratch*.
scrawl: To climb awkwardly sideways. Cf. scrawl: crab (Lincs.).
scrip: A shepherd's coat, generally made of leather.
scrowed: Marked or scratched, in lines.
shattered: Sprinkled; scattered.
shill: Shrill.
shoaf: Sheaf.
shool: To saunter lazily.
shoves: Sheaves.
shoy: Shy.
sicken: To mope.
sinkfoil: Cinquefoil, probably *Potentilla reptans*.
skewish: Inclined to shy.
slive: To slide or slip past.
slove: Pret. of *slive*.
sluther: To slide, slither.
small swipes: small beer.
snob: A shoemaker or cobbler.
snuft: To snuffle or sniff.
soodle: To saunter.
spirey: Pointed and tapering, like a spire.
sprent: Sprinkled.
sprotes: Small twigs, for firewood.
sputter: To run up quickly, with a commotion.
startle: To start, as in surprise, to be in a great bustle.
stick: To decorate.

stingo: Strong ale or beer.

stiver: A coin of small value.

stools: The exposed roots of trees.

stouk: Stook.

stoven: Stump of a tree.

stowk: Stook.

streak. To stretch.

strime: To stride.

strinkle: To scatter, sprinkle.

on the strunt: Strutting.

struttle: Minnow or stickleback.

stulp: Stump.

stunt: Steep, sharp.

sturnel: Starling.

sturt: To start, to shake suddenly.

sutty: Clare's spelling of sooty.

swail: Swale, shade.

swath: A range or row of cut grass or corn, as it falls from the scythe.

swea: See *swee*.

swee: Swaying, rocking. Cf. see-saw.

swift: This word occurs later in the selection and refers to the same creature, the common newt or eft.

swoof: Var. of sough—deep sigh, or breath.

swop: To swoop or pounce.

taws: Marbles.

teem: To empty, to pour out.

then: Clare's consistent form of *than*.

throstle: The song-thrush or missel-thrush.

trace: To walk.

tray: Hurdle.

trepid: Fearful.

tutle: Clare's spelling of *tootle*.

twank: A shorter, sharper variant of *twang*.

unbrunt: Unaffected or untouched by the assault or brunt.

watchet: Sky blue.

water-blab: Water-blob, marsh marigold.

wear: To persevere in.

were: Clare's almost consistent spelling of *where*.

wetting: Whetting.

whew: The cry of the owl.

while: Until.

whimpling: Wimpling, rippling, meandering.
wift: Whift, or whiff; a puff of smoke as from a pipe.
wimble: A gimlet or auger.
winnow: To beat the air.
without side: On the outside.

yaum: Var. of yealm, a prepared layer of wetted straw for thatching, about eighteen inches by five inches.
yaumd: (Of beans): cut carefully and gathered into a manageable sheaf of about the same size and shape as a thatcher's yealm.
yoe: Ewe.
younker: Youngster.

INDEX OF FIRST LINES